THE TAMAR

Cover: Midsuummmer Tamar from North Hooe to Cotehele Quay

*The unhurried, mature Tamar musing through
a gentle landscape near Horse Bridge*

WEST COUNTRY RIVERS

The TAMAR

A Great Little River

Rob Furneaux

EX LIBRIS PRESS

First published in 1992 by
Ex Libris Press
1 The Shambles
Bradford on Avon
Wiltshire

Typeset in 10 point Palatino

Design and typesetting by Ex Libris Press

Cover printed by Shires Press, Trowbridge
Printed and bound in Great Britain by
Dotesios Ltd., Trowbridge, Wiltshire

ISBN 9 948578 39 4

To my father: a man of the River Yealm

CONTENTS

Acknowledgements

I would like to acknowledge the kind help and assistance of all those who contributed towards the writing of this book. Particular thanks are due to Gordon West of Dunterton, who sadly passed away in September 1991. Thanks are also due to Ray White and Jenny Griffiths of the N.R.A., and Gary Emerson of Morwellham – all of whom provided me with valuable information. I would also like to thank the authorities at St. Mellion Country Club who provided a mass of statistics and literature about their club; also Mike Summers of Launceston Angler's Association, Terry Wood of Horse Bridge, Chris Goodall of the Tamar Protection Society, and Audrey Wheatley of The Bude Canal Society – all of whom helped to fill gaps in my knowledge. A debt of gratitude is due to the long suffering staffs of Tavistock and Plymouth libraries whom I pestered for well hidden articles on several occasions. Mention should also be made of Bob Phillips who gave advice on word processing and criticism of my first draft (too much for my liking!)

Finally my thanks to Dave Arnold and Barbara Furneaux for undertaking the tedious proof reading and correcting my eccentric spelling and, of course, to my publisher Roger Jones who roped me into the idea of a Tamar book in the first place.

Rob Furneaux
Bere Ferrers
June 1992

Introduction

The River Tamar is one of the great rivers of the world. An overstatement? No, I don't think so. Let's examine the facts: first of all there is the name Tamar; it certainly has a rather majestic air to it. 'Tamar' seems naturally to lend itself to be categorised alongside the Thames, the Severn, and other great rivers with majestic sounding names. Indeed, the derivation of 'Tamar' itself is 'Great Water'.

'Tamar' seems almost synonymous with all the good things which people associate with the names 'The West Country' and 'Devon and Cornwall'. Thatched cottages, sleepy fishing villages, Dartmoor, Exmoor and Tamar seem to fit well into a sense of tranquil well-being. To look at things another way, I am not so sure I would have raised quite as much enthusiasm for writing about one of Dorset's most important rivers: 'The Piddle'.

So, before looking any further, we can establish that the Tamar is a great river by title at least. Hopefully, as you read on, I'll be able to convince you that the Tamar is not a great river by name only. On the face of it this is quite a challenge in itself.

The River Thames, for instance, is not a very long river by international standards, but its greatness stems largely from historical associations rather than geographical considerations. The Tamar, though smaller, also has a rich and varied human history upon its banks.

Historically, mention of the name Tamar (or Tamare) goes back to the days of Ptolemy in the second century, where it is mentioned in his series of books entitled *Geographike Huphegesis*. Although sounding grand, these books are only of passing interest today. Some of Ptolemy's conclusions are seen as slightly dubious, for instance, that the Nile has its source somewhere on the mountains of the moon.

From source to sea the Tamar is a mere 72 kilometres in length;in comparison, the Thames has a length of 350 kilometres. It cannot be denied that in this respect the Tamar must be considered as the tiniest of tiddlers. It has a lot of ground to make up to prove it is a river of any stature at all.

In comparison with the Thames, the Tamar can establish pre-eminence in one department straight away. The Thames estuary is surrounded by a flat, largely featureless landscape dominated for the most part by the sprawling built-up area of London. The Tamar's estuary, conversely, is cradled within a rich and varied landscape of deciduous woodland, verdant rolling hills and precipitous rocky slopes cascading to the river's edge.

Taking its length into account, the Tamar can perhaps be described as a 'potted' great river. It has many attributes you would expect to find in connection with many a great river, the only difference being that the Tamar contains these attributes in a compact and concentrated way.

What are these attributes? Well, let's start with its location: any great river worth its salt must, for at least part of its length, perform the task of being an international boundary separating diverse nations and cultures. The Tamar certainly performs this function, it divides Devon from Cornwall for the greater part of its length. Wait a minute I hear you say, Devon and Cornwall are only counties, not countries. You try telling that to a Cornishman! To a Cornishman, the county is nothing less than an independent state with its own customs, language, and identity. The fact that Cornwall remains part of the U.K. is merely because the Cornish have a generous and forgiving nature that precludes them from wanting to cause too much of a commotion with the English – or at least that's what a Cornishman will tell you. Also, there's a lot more English than Cornish.

Historically, Cornwall was for a time an independent state with the Tamar marking the international boundary. Needless to say, this is not within living memory. The county appears to have been in-dependent for various periods up until the end of the tenth century.

The Cornish seem to have done their best to maintain their fragile independence, even going to the extent of enlisting the help of outside allies. On one occasion (838 AD) the Danes navigated the Tamar to a place near where Calstock now stands (called the Danescombe Valley), and gave the Cornish a hand against the invading Saxons. The battle which ensued, at Hingston Down, two miles from the

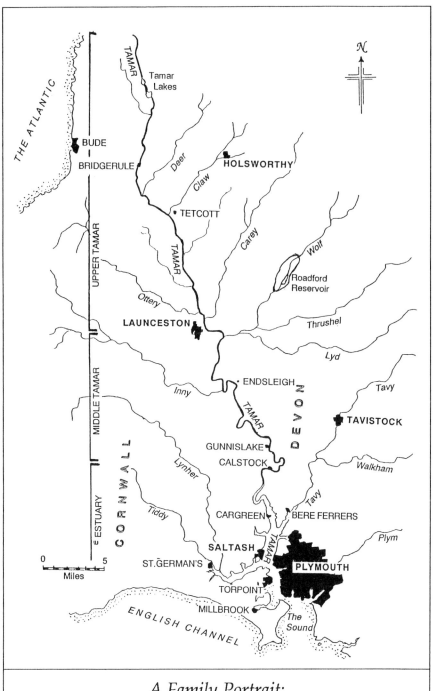

A Family Portrait:
The Tamar and her Tributaries

Tamar, was a decisive defeat, but the Saxons were a little tardy in advancing further westward beyond the river, and in 936 AD King Athelstan officially established the Tamar as the boundary between the Celtic Cornish and the Saxon English. The tiny Cornish state was too small to survive for long; little by little, Saxon incursions reached further and further down the peninsula. Gradually, Cornwall began to fall under the jurisdiction of the Saxons from England. Indeed, by the time of William the Conqueror's reign, Cornwall was firmly in English hands.

I suppose I should place my cards on the table at the outset and state that I'm a Devonian born and bred and, for no logical reason, Devonians have always been slightly wary of the Cornish. I don't subscribe to that attitude, but whilst researching this book I've always been a little apprehensive of being caught on the Cornish bank of the river after dark. In truth, I have got nothing against the Cornish and Cornwall; after all, if their country never existed, I'd be writing about a stretch of coastline.

The Tamar road bridge (left) and Brunel's Royal Albert Bridge (right) dominate the river at Saltash

Besides being a very important boundary, the Tamar bears comparison with great rivers in other ways. Many great rivers have important or impressive bridges spanning their waters; the Tamar has one as well. The 'Royal Albert' rail bridge crossing the river at Saltash is one of the most interesting rail bridges anywhere in the world. I admit it is nothing like as long as the Humber Road Bridge or the bridge across the Tagus at Lisbon, but until the completion of the Dartford Bridge it was longer than anything across the Thames.

The Tamar has its fair share of great houses and castles along its course; they are not quite as well known as Windsor Castle for instance, but they are none the worse for that. Great houses, like Cotehele on the Tamar estuary, thrive in their intimacy and comparative seclusion – and you're unlikely to find any of these filled to the gunwales with Japanese tourists.

Some great rivers, like the the Plate and the St.Lawrence, have been canalised successfully, and their waters have been used to open up vast tracts of the interior of great land masses. The Tamar has this too: the Bude Canal – but perhaps I'm stretching a point here; the tub boats of the canal were never quite on a par with the huge ore carriers of the St. Lawrence. Nevertheless, to look at it another way, great canals, like the Panama Canal, were projects which looked for a time as if they would never be completed but eventually were pushed through from coast to coast. The builders of the Bude Canal, however, never did see their dream of connecting the north and south coasts of Cornwall fulfilled. Who knows, even the great canal builder de Lesseps might have failed were he to have tried.

The Tamar has had its fair share of success. The development of the great naval base at Devonport must be high on the list. For centuries it has harboured 'The Wooden Walls of England' (and Cornwall) and has stood as a staunch sentinel against the threat of invasion. Many an enemy has known too well that while Devonport remained a safe haven, the western channel could not be crossed by any invasion fleet. In respect of defending the realm the Tamar bears the word great without question.

Many great rivers of the world have great cities at their mouths; the Hudson has New York, while the Thames has London. The Tamar in its turn has Plymouth (Devonport being part of the city). Plymouth, like the Tamar, may not be as large as some of its rivals, but it certainly makes up for it with a long and illustrious history. Over the centuries many an expedition has left the port, many of which have done much to change the course of world history. Much of the exploration and colonisation of the Americas, Australia and New Zealand was undertaken by expeditions which set out from Plymouth Sound.

Without the Tamar, there would be no Plymouth Sound. Plymouth Sound is largely a product of erosion which occurred during the great ice ages. At those times, sea levels dropped considerably; consequently the Tamar did not reach the sea until a position somewhere beyond where Plymouth Breakwater now stands. When sea levels rose again the Tamar's channel, and that of its tributary the Plym, became the basis of what we now know as Plymouth Sound.

Another claim for the Tamar to be a great river comes from a rather unlikely quarter – the media. A few years ago the ubiquitous children's programme *Blue Peter* produced a series of 'Blue Peter Special Assignments'. Some of these programmes were devoted to 'Great Rivers'. Having surveyed such minor streams as the Amazon, they eventually produced a programme devoted to the Tamar, and spent almost an hour following the river's course from source to sea. So, in the eyes of 'Blue Peter' at least, the Tamar has indeed achieved greatness, and I for one would not dare to challenge anything that has been said on *Blue Peter*.

If the Tamar has achieved any sort of greatness, some of it must be due to the waters of the river which have been generously donated by a host of tributaries. To put it in theatrical terms, no large-scale production totally succeeds without a good supporting cast. The Tamar's list of supporting players is a long one. The major tributaries are quite an impressive cast list within themselves: The Tavy, Carey, Thrushel, Lynher, Inny, Ottery, Claw, Lyd, and Deer; all important rivers on a local scale. The fact that the Tamar becomes a wide and majestic waterway in its lower course is in no small part due to the millions of gallons added to the river by these and a host of lesser streams.

In total, the Tamar and its family of tributaries drain more than 700 square kilometres of Devon and Cornwall. In the West, the head waters of the Lynher dispute the draining of Bodmin Moor with the River Fowey. In the East, long sinuous fingers of the Tavy stretch upwards towards the highest summits of Dartmoor whilst, in the

The Tamar tributary – the River Tiddy – with its elegant railway viaduct taking the main line into deepest Cornwall!

north, emissaries of the Inny and the Ottery seem almost to snatch their waters from the lofty clifftops of North Cornwall, carrying them off as captive prizes for the Tamar.

There is little doubt that in the area of land it drains the Tamar is pre-eminent in the south-west. But for me it goes further than that; the Tamar is one of *the* Great Rivers. Some rivers can be described as great because they drain vast areas or have a length of many hundreds of miles, but does a river have to be big to be great? The Tamar has everything a great river should have, but in concentrated form; the very fact that the Tamar manages so many things in so small an area, for me, only adds to the attraction.

The infant Tamar struggles to life amongst the coarse undergrowth of Woolley Moor

1
A Little Stream amongst the Bracken

Fount of rushing water wild flowers wreath
the home where thy first waters sunlight claims.
The lark sits hushed beside thee while I breathe
sweet tamar's spring! The music of thy name.
Depths that give back the soft eyed violets gaze,
shores whence tall navies march to meet the tide,
O Tamar flow, lowly I bend mine ear,
and listen to thy lisp that greets the shore,
Bearing traditions further soft and clear,
from the dim portals of the never more.

Carrington (1777 - 1830)

High amongst the windswept moorland of North Cornwall, where the stunted trees bend their backs to the howl of Atlantic winter gales, there trickles a tiny stream. It weaves its way amongst thickets of gorse and bracken seemingly struggling to maintain a path through the morass of undergrowth. I journeyed here for the first time some years back. I remember that it was a chill November day; a thick west country mist had descended over the high hills. I had come on a solitary pilgrimage to find the source of the Tamar. The Ordnance Survey map told me I would find it at a place called Woolley Moor, a location just a little over three and a half miles from the north Cornish coast .

I parked the car on the little lonely road between Woolley Barrows and the isolated hamlet of East Youlstone. The bleak moorland had not yet become the quagmire it always does with the onset of winter. The ground was comparatively dry underfoot so I unhesitatingly plunged into the undergrowth to do battle with the thistles and the thorn thickets in my quest to find the very place where the rivulet rises. Eventually, with stinging fingers and aching ankles, but with my spirits undampened, I found a little gully in the turf; it was only about nine inches wide, and dropped about a foot from the level of the coarse undergrowth. I rejoiced. I had found what was undoubtedly the source of the Tamar!

Eagerly, I extracted my camera from my camera bag, removed the lens cap, and prepared to record this holy place. The little gully was however dry, its bed strewn with the last of the windblown leaves of autumn – an irony I thought; they were dying at the very place where the Tamar was being given life. I moved from one side to the other looking for the best place to take the shot. I came to the conclusion that it would be best if I put one foot on the stream bed and took a picture directly along its course. I put a foot onto the leaves and sank almost instantly to my knee in mud, at the same time taking an involuntary picture of my trouser leg.

The Tamar was alive and kicking. Many's the time when I've been boating on the Tamar estuary some forty miles to the south, and have stepped from the boat to be greeted by a boot full of mud; the place

Stunted trees bend their backs to Atlantic gales near the Tamar's source.

I'd expected to get covered in mud was here. It seemed as though the Tamar in her infancy was playing childish games with me. If the Tamar is somehow a living entity – I know it's illogical, but that's how it sometimes seems to me – then I could almost hear it giggling impishly with the success of its little deception.

The place where the Tamar springs to life is a location of no great natural beauty. It has no impressively massive tors dominating the landscape like Dartmoor, neither can it be likened to the verdant rolling hills of South Devon. This is a high windswept plateau largely devoid of farmland, and inhabited by stunted trees and wiry undergrowth. In winter, the wind howls in from the sea for days on end, and it has been said that anyone who comes here needs a man beside him to hold his hat on.

Somehow, regardless of the sombre bleakness, this seems a magical and mysterious place. The location has more of an affinity with the coast than with the interior. Places like Boscastle and Tintagel are just a few miles away, and the whole of this area is steeped in the legend of King Arthur. It is fascinating to conjecture whether this almost immortal monarch used the Tamar as a defence line against his dangerous neighbours. Well, we all know that the Arthur legend is far too imprecise to be reliably pinned down to any particular location, but it is a delicious thought to imagine the infant Tamar as a site where gallant knights of the court rested their horses to drink from the pure waters. Here I am soaring away on flights of fancy, but I can think of few rivers whose location suggests a connection with the legend as plausibly as the Tamar.

The Tamar has a legend of its own, and like all good legends its origins lie languishing deep in obscurity. There was once, many centuries ago, a nymph called Tamara who lived in the underworld. She didn't seem to like the underworld very much and took to exploring the world above.

One day she chanced upon two giants called Tavy and Torridge – or Tawradge, Of course both of them instantly fell in love with her. Being a rather flighty young thing, she decided to lead them both on, and refused to choose between them. Eventually, they insisted that she make a choice. Meanwhile, Tamara's parents were becoming somewhat anxious, and were wondering where she had gone. Her father was dispatched to find her. After a while he discovered her fraternising with the two unknown giants. At this, he flew into an uncontrollable rage (threw a wobbly) and put a spell on both the giants, sending them into a deep sleep. Tamara, somewhat miffed that her two new boyfriends had been suddenly rendered inoperative, refused to accompany her father back to the underworld. At this, he became even more angry, and in a fit of temper (which I'm sure he regretted afterwards) he turned his daughter into a river.

Tamara had been a beautiful thing; the new river echoed her elegance, and calmly and majestically made its way to the sea.

What of the two giants? Well, Tavy soon awoke, and was heart-broken that he had lost his new found love. He approached his father, who also was a weaver of magic spells, and asked his advice. His father realised that the only thing for it was to turn Tavy into a river too, and send him off in search of Tamara. Eventually he found her, and together they turned into a wide and beautiful estuary as they merged with one another.

Torridge had woken also, and had sought the advice of a wise magician (it seems there were a lot of them about in those days). He too was turned into a river, and wandered the countryside in a vain search for Tamara. Eventually, he gave up and turned north towards the north Devon coast, never again to set eyes upon the beautiful Tamara.

The legend of Tamara certainly explains why the River Torridge, which rises a mere 500 metres from the Tamar, turns away from the Tamar in a huge arc and eventually flows to the North Devon coast. I'm not sure if geographers accept this particular reason for the Torridge's unusual course.

Before leaving the source of the Tamar, mention should be made of another river, the Marsland Water. This river is no more than a little stream, and has a length of only about three miles from source to sea. The Marsland Water, however, has an important role to play; it shares the Devon / Cornwall border with the Tamar and covers most of the distance from the Tamar's source to the Atlantic. The distance between both rivers' head waters is less than two miles.

If you go to see the Tamar's source it is well worth a detour to take a look at the little Marsland Water and its near neighbour the Welcombe. Both have superbly unspoilt valleys which spectacularly reach a coastline where towering cliffs are constantly under attack from the relentless Atlantic swell. The Marsland Water is such a small stream that even when it reaches the coast one foot can easily be put on either bank. It is not advisable to try a similar experiment where the Tamar reaches the sea at the other end of the border. In less than a mile from its humble beginnings on Woolley Moor, the fledgling Tamar has created a small valley in which to hide from rigorous North Cornwall winters. In this valley can be found the first bridge across the river – between East and West Youlstone Farms; the Tamar flowing beneath is little more than a rivulet. The bridge is not a large one, but simply a one foot diameter pipe with a country lane passing over it. Nevertheless, for the first time there is a sign proclaiming the boundary. This sign, on the eastern bank, proudly displays the word 'Devon'. The Cornish, perhaps surprisingly, have made no response on their bank.

For the next mile and a half the little Tamar stream heads southward through farmland which is becoming increasingly fertile as the river drops towards the 150 metre contour. There are two further bridges at Youlstone Ham and at Buse's Mill – both are rather miniature affairs. Suddenly the scene changes. The little stream surrenders its scurrying waters into a large and placid lake. This is the first of the two 'Tamar Lakes'. The name itself seems to have an almost magical ring to it. Was this the place where, long ago, in the midst of the dark ages, Excalibur was thrust upwards out of the limpid waters of a dark lake? Was this the place where a dying king consigned his trusty sword to reside for an eternity? Have the swirling mists of time hidden a long lost connection with King Arthur's immortal legend? Well, frankly, no. The lakes are both reservoirs supplying an area of North Cornwall. This is not as bad as it sounds; these are not the massive, impersonal and sterile water repositories which many modern reservoirs seem to be. The Tamar Lakes may not have any long lost historical connections, but they are a very pleasant place to come to sail, fish, and walk beside.

The upper of the two lakes is of most recent origin, and was completed in 1975. It supplies water to a fifteen mile wide coastal strip stretching from Crackington Haven to Hartland. The lower lake is rather older, having been completed in 1822, and started life as a feeder reservoir for the Bude Canal (more about this later). At neither lake will you be encountering a major engineering masterpiece.

The modern dam impounding Upper Tamar Lake

However, both lakes are to be described as extremely significant in a completely different context. Year after year a large number of people visit the lakes. They arrive often in a state of excitement, and nearly always with a great sense of anticipation. What are they coming here for? The answer is they're hoping for a close encounter of the bird kind.

The Tamar Lakes are a paradise for the bird watcher. In this part of North Devon and Cornwall there are few areas of permanent standing water. Geese and other water-loving birds flock to the lakes in great numbers. Sometimes it is almost as though they are queuing up to find a piece of vacant water. The Lakes offer sanctuary to many species, these include shovelers, pintails, jack snipe, curlews, green sandpipers, wood sandpipers, and many others. A local speciality is the gadwell which is a graceful bird looking rather like a slim mallard. At the beginning and end of the year the lakes are also the home of the majestic Bewick's Swan.

Most commonly resident upon the lake, especially in the winter months, are large numbers of ducks. About a hundred mallard utilise the sheltered waters, as do up to two hundred widgeon; a similar number of teals invariably arrive in the early autumn. During the savage winter storms, when the nearby Atlantic coast becomes a cauldron of howling fury, even robust herring gulls seek shelter on these perennially placid waters.

The Lakes area is also the home of predator species; overhead on still mornings one may often spot the sleek shape of a peregrine or merlin, patiently circling in search of prey.

Facilities for twitchers (bird watchers) are good at the Lakes. There is a bird hide, permits for which can be obtained at the Upper Lake Office. A bird log book is kept at the warden's building and information centre. I'm told that the Tamar Lakes provide one of the best locations to bird watch in the south-west of England, which itself is a very important area. Here, the lakes are comparable only with Slapton Ley, Stithians Reservoir, the Isles of Scilly, and Crowdy Reservoir for the number and variety of birds which can be seen. The importance of the Lower Lake is reflected in the fact that it was designated a bird sanctuary in 1951.

Such importance means that American tourists are sometimes seen at the Tamar Lakes; but these are not the types who wear cameras like jewellery around their necks, and specialise in loud shirts. No, these are American birds which are blown off course from the eastern seaboard of the U.S.A. and Canada by strong prevailing westerlies, and find themselves in Britain. Such visitors include pectoral sandpipers and long-billed dowitchers. Fortunately, the Foreign Office seems to have no plans to eject them as illegal immigrants.

The Upper Lake caters for sailing enthusiasts who, like the herring gulls, prefer to drift calmly around the lake rather than risk the unshackled elements sometimes evident along the coast. Pleasant paths have been laid out to walk around both lakes and from the Lower Lake another path leads southward for two miles following the line of the Bude Canal.

Both lakes are very popular with the angling fraternity, the Lower Lake is well stocked with tench, rudd, carp, and bream. Bream in particular have thrived in the lake; in 1983 the population exploded for no apparent reason, and it was possible to catch over one hundred pounds of them in one daily session. The Upper Lake, meanwhile, specialises in trout.

A quiet fishing location beside Lower Tamar Lake

As far as the Lower Lake is concerned a debt of gratitude is owed to the South West Water Authority. In 1978 it was withdrawn from use (having been superseded by the Upper Lake). New regulations concerning earth dams meant that it would either have to be substantially strengthened, or demolished. In their wisdom South West Water decided to do the necessary work and keep the lake alive.

The Lakes, nourished by the fledgling Tamar, remain a haven for birds, fish, and those who would watch and catch them. Commercialisation has not yet reached this quiet corner of the west country – long may it remain so.

Virworthy Wharf and the Bude Canal

2

The Middle Reaches:
a West Country Suez Unfulfilled

Thanks to the South West Water Authority, the Lower Tamar Lake survives intact. As the Tamar emerges from beneath its earth dam it is accompanied by another small waterway but, unlike the lake, this is a mere relic of former times. A tow-path remains, alongside which languishes a muddy reed-filled ditch, its waters clouded and unmoving, a stark contrast to the nearby rushing and tumbling Tamar, freed from the confines of the Lake.

The reed-filled ditch is all that remains of the once industrious Bude Canal which carried barges from the coast at Bude far into the interior of Devon and Cornwall. A hundred years ago this proud little waterway transported cargoes as far as Holsworthy in the East, and Druxton near Launceston in the south.

It might seem a strange notion to build an expensive canal across the centre of this, one of the most underpopulated parts of the west country. It passes through no large towns; neither did it terminate at anywhere of importance. This was an essentially agricultural waterway passing through farmland, and catering to the needs of farmers. Its chief cargo was nothing more spectacular than sand, but sand which was vital to improve the poor acidic soils of the area.

It had long been recognised that the calcium-rich sand of the North Cornwall Coast greatly increased the fertility of the soils and, as far back as the fourteenth century, it had been transported by the monks of Tavistock Abbey as far south as Werrington (some twelve miles from the coast). Transport was by pack horse along narrow trackways, the toil and trouble of which can only be imagined.

In 1774 a Cornishman, John Edyvean, made public the idea of constructing a canal to transport the sand inland. His was a grand scheme envisaging a waterway cutting right across the peninsula to join the tidal Tamar at Weir Head near Gunnislake. An Act enabling the canal's construction was duly passed on the 24th May that year. As with many large-scale projects, things were not as straightforward as they looked. The distance between Bude and Gunnislake is only twenty-five miles, but the surveyed route was a tortuous total of ninety miles. It wriggled through the countryside avoiding almost every possible obstruction. Perhaps partly because of this fact, sufficient money for Edyvean's scheme could not be raised, and nothing was done.

Next onto the scene came John Smeaton – the architect of the third Eddystone lighthouse. He considered the county of Cornwall to be almost incompatible with the building of canals, due to its irregular, hilly terrain and suggested that the best way to build a waterway would be to canalise the Tamar itself, using a system incorporating two inclined planes and sixteen or more locks.

Again no action was taken, and not one shovel was lifted in anger. Perhaps in this case it was fortunate. Had the Tamar been confined and tamed, much of its beauty would surely have been compromised, and the free-flowing spirit of its waters extinguished. Recently, I visited the Thames at Windsor – a very pleasant spot – but the old river is cruelly manacled and caged by its locks, whilst its banks are adorned with boating notices declaring 'No Waiting','Private' and even 'Keep Right'. Pity the poor Tamar had she met with a similar fate.

The survey game continued: in 1785 the route was investigated by an engineer named Leach. He suggested a revised version of a plan by Smeaton, but this scheme also sank without trace. Next came the Nuttall plan in the 1790's; it detailed a waterway joining Morwellham near Calstock with the village of North Tamerton some way north of Launceston. No action was taken on this plan either.

The following name in the survey queue was that of Robert Fulton – the architect of much of Devonoport's civic splendour. He mused upon the project for three years and, although he had some good ideas, on this occasion nothing got further than the drawing board.

In 1814 two gentlemen of Bridgerule Parish, called Harward and Braddon, tried to revive interest in the scheme. The Napoleonic War was raging at the time, and this soon put a damper on things. 1817 dawned and Thomas Shearm and James Green joined the long list

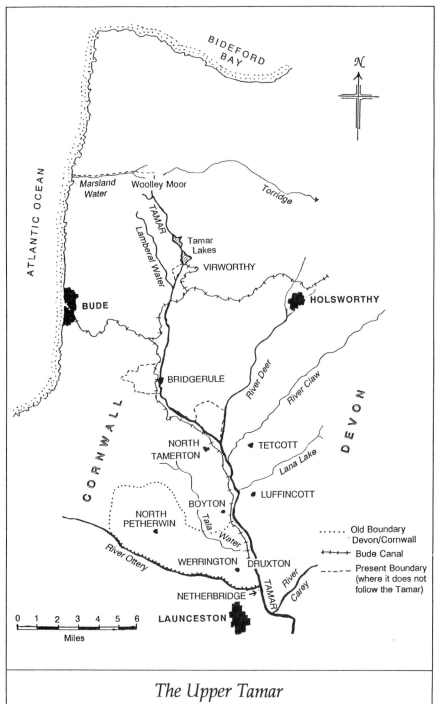

BIDEFORD BAY

Torridge

ATLANTIC OCEAN

Marsland Water

Woolley Moor

TAMAR

Lamberal Water

Tamar Lakes

VIRWORTHY

BUDE

HOLSWORTHY

River Deer

River Claw

BRIDGERULE

CORNWALL

DEVON

NORTH TAMERTON

TETCOTT

Lana Lake

LUFFINCOTT

BOYTON

NORTH PETHERWIN

Tala Water

River Ottery

WERRINGTON

DRUXTON

TAMAR

River Carey

NETHERBRIDGE

LAUNCESTON

.... Old Boundary Devon/Cornwall

┼┼┼┼┼ Bude Canal

------ Present Boundary (where it does not follow the Tamar)

0 1 2 3 4 5 6
Miles

The Upper Tamar and Middle Reaches

of interested parties. Their plan was grandiose in the extreme, and foresaw a complete canal system with extensions to South Molton, Tiverton, Exeter, Bideford (and Timbuktu no doubt). Although the overall plan was ambitious, the section from Bude to Launceston seemed feasible. A survey of parishes along the canal's route indicated that a healthy profit could be made from the carriage of sand alone. Funding the project would no longer be a stumbling block.

With building costs estimated at £128,341, a Canal Committee went to Parliament to obtain another bill (1819) and the Bude Harbour and Canal Company was set up. At last, discussion had ended and work could proceed.

On 23rd July 1819 the first sod was cut at Bude, whilst construction started almost simultaneously at several points along the route. Work went ahead at speed. Moreover, the labour force seem to have had the unusual problem of being too industrious. It wasn't long before claims for damages began appearing from those resident alongside the canal's course. They complained that their crops had been trampled, or their animals had strayed because the provision for canalside fencing was not as efficiently dealt with as the building of the canal itself. One of the more expensive claims amounted to a total of two pounds ten shillings.

By 1823 the canal had been completed from Bude to Holsworthy; and from the newly built Tamar Lake – which supplied the canal water – to North Tamerton. A year later it had reached as far south as Druxton, three miles from Launceston. This was a total distance, including the branch to Holsworthy, of 35.5 miles.

Here building ceased. The canal was not to cover those few extra miles which would have connected it with the tide at Gunnislake. Had it reached Gunnislake, its importance would have undoubtedly greatly increased, and who knows, it might still be in existence today. Why was it not completed? The answer seems partly to be buried deep in the English class system.

After reaching Druxton, the canal's course was to have followed the Tamar on its way south to Launceston. This took the waterway through land belonging to the Duke of Northumberland. The Duke was not against the idea, but in 1818 the promoters of the canal had suddenly produced a map showing the route of the canal going across the Duke's parkland and right in front of his mansion. At such an idea, the poor old Duke threw a fit, and refused any canal building at all on his land. To make things worse, the chief promoter of the canal project was Earl Stanhope. In the pecking order of the peerage Dukes beat Earls every time, and the poor Earl was in no position to fight the wishes of his superior.

As completed, the canal was, nevertheless, quite an achievement. Sand and other goods were transported in 'Tub Boats'. These were square barges measuring twenty feet by five feet six inches. Each could carry twenty tons of sand. The journey from Bude began, like most canals, with a water course interspersed with locks. However, when the canal reached Marmchurch, some two miles inland, the barges were carried uphill on an inclined plane; for this purpose the barges were fitted with small fourteen-inch diameter wheels.

One of the few tangible remains of the Bude Canal. The little aqueduct over the Tala Water – just north of Druxton.

The inclined plane was an ingenious invention. The Canal engineers utilised two different lifting devices for these. One operated using two huge iron buckets of ten feet in diameter suspended into deep shafts`. When a bucket was filled with water it would be allowed

*The youthful Tamar near Dexbeer shortly after its escape
from Lower Tamar Lake*

to slowly descend the shaft, its weight drawing a loaded barge up the incline by means of a continuous chain. Once it had reached the bottom (and the barge the top) the water would be discharged and the bucket drawn up by the weight of the other, now filled bucket, coming down.

Between Bude and Druxton there were a total of five inclined planes to negotiate; one used the bucket method whilst the other four operated on a slightly different system, using a rotating water-wheel with a chain attached to draw up the barges.

In theory this system was ingenious, in practice there were often breakdowns. These usually happened when the incline chains parted. The sound of one of the huge buckets crashing to the bottom of its shaft was said to be, 'terrific, and if once heard never forgotten'. In reality, the conception of the canal was far beyond the materials used to construct it.

The canal banks were often damaged when barges were blown off course by a sudden breeze. With the pulling horse unable to restrain them they would crash into the fragile earth and clay banks.

There is little doubt that the resident clerk in charge of the canal's operation had a continuous headache. There were human frailties to deal with too. John Honey, clerk from 1824 to 1832, reported one such case in his diary. He had been told of an engineer who was repairing the canal sides using the highly unsatisfactory method of cob walling (mud and stones). His labourers knew it was wrong and tried to tell him; he answered (according to the diary):

> Let it be right or wrong. Do as I tell you, then you'll have no fault". And when they would say they thought it would not (do) he would say in answer, "d * * n thee; thee has no right to think, for I am paid for thinking, and thee for working. Therefore, do as I tell thee or be off."

As we all know, people of that persuasion are not unique to the nineteenth century.

At harvest time when sand was not needed, annual maintenance was attended to, whilst in the winter the canal was kept open during hard frosts by a horse-drawn ice breaker boat.

For the greater part of the century the canal faithfully served the little farming communities along its route. At its zenith in the 1840's more than one hundred people were employed by the company. As with so many canals, it was the coming of the railway which spelt the end. In 1864 the tracks reached Launceston; by 1879 Holsworthy had a rail connection. For a while the company continued trading; but nobody had any illusions, it would lose the rest of its trade when the railway reached Bude. The section following the Tamar to Druxton line was closed in November 1891. Discussion about the fate of other portions of the canal continued until 1901 when the company was finally wound up. Sections of the canal were sold piece-meal to local farmers, whilst Stratton Rural District Council took over the picturesque Bude section, and also Tamar Lake for use as a reservoir serving the Bude area.

The Bude Canal followed the Tamar for more than seventeen miles of its length. A much quoted poem about rivers states; 'men may come and men may go, but I go on for ever.' It holds true in this case; the Tamar flows on as always, but of the man-made Bude Canal, hardly a trace remains. Following its closure, the land it occupied was largely ploughed under, its bridges dismantled, and its tub boats burnt as firewood or abandoned to rot.

Today, very little evidence remains. The Exeter Maritime Museum have in their possession a tub boat as part of a Bude Canal exhibit. The course of the canal can be recognised by its towpath in some places; alongside it, milestones are occasionally seen. Virworthy Wharf at the head of the Canal near Tamar Lake has been the subject of some restoration, the basin having now been cleared of sediment and weed; a nature reserve and walk has been created between the wharf and the Lower Tamar lake.

The walk from Lower Tamar Lake to Virworthy Wharf is a particularly pleasant one with glimpses of the fledgling Tamar to one side and the remains of the old canal to the other. Along most of this stretch the canal still holds water, but has long been choked by reeds and sedges. Along its course old bollards can occasionally be located. At Virworthy Wharf there is now a little museum located in an old stone barn. Here is a wealth of information to guide you on your walk.

Much of the rest of the course of the canal is now in private hands and cannot be visited by the public; but where it is crossed by public

Iron marker stone alongside the remains of the Bude Canal

roads the dry bed can be seen in a few places. One such site is at Tamartown, two miles north of Werrington, where evidence of the Werrington Incline can be seen as it crosses over a road. Another is located one mile north-east of Werrington. Here, a small aqueduct over Tala Water, a Tamar tributary, can be seen from the road.

Recently, The Bude Canal Society has been formed with the aim of clearing canalside walks, and undertaking restoration projects. For most of its length however, the canal lies vanquished, its scant remains the victim of nature's endless assault. Winter frosts fragment surviving stone work while summer's soft green tendrils inexorably obscure its course. Below in the valley, the Tamar flows quietly onward, content that a pretender to its crown lies abandoned by the hand that created it.

The Tamar near East Balsdon (two miles south of Bridgerule).
A tranquil picture of well watered pasture land, typical
of much of the upper third of the Tamar.

3

The Middle Reaches:
the Stream becomes a River
and a Boundary Dispute

After its escape from the clutches of the Lower Tamar Lake, the river once more resumes a southward course. The pace is an unhurried one; the little stream seems content to amble its way through a mellow landscape characterised by a patchwork of fields interspersed with thickets of trees and isolated farm houses. There is no deep rumble of cascading water, no hissing of spray as restless waters crash their way through a harsh and boulder-infested landscape. As her name suggests, the Tamar is a placid and unhurried being. She is not yet mature, but already her countenance is stately and her manners refined. Anyone of such good-natured habits must surely attract a gallery of devoted friends; the Tamar is no exception. Within barely a mile of the Lake the stream is joined by the first of a host of tributaries. This is the Lamberal Water, a brook whose source may be found high on the Cornish Moors amongst a cluster of tumuli and other mysteriously haunting stone monuments of the Iron Age.

Even with the assistance of the Lamberal Water, the Tamar remains little more than a tiny stream. The average daily flow of the river at this point is barely three square meters per second – a trickle by anyone's standards.

A mile onward finds the Tamar passing beneath another remnant of the past, the lonely and derelict Burmsden aqueduct. It stands as a defiant monument to those who toiled in the building of the Bude Canal.

A little further on and the first important road bridge reached. This is the A3072, a major artery of the tourist trade. In summer, it is packed with cars and caravans on the way to the coast. Motorists speeding past are unlikely to catch a glimpse of the little Tamar beneath. Only the signs confronting each other with the names 'Devon' and 'Cornwall' give any indication that the Tamar passes quietly below the straight unaltering course of the road.

With the hum of traffic ebbing away behind it, the Tamar heads out into quiet countryside. For the next fifteen miles the river is to flow through some of the most thinly populated farming land in the two counties. There are no towns, the only settlements are small isolated hamlets – usually a church and a small cluster of houses with rarely even a pub.

The first village encountered is Bridgerule. This is one of the oldest bridging points of the Tamar. Records of a bridge on this site reach back to the eleventh century. A pre-Roman trackway is also said to have crossed the river here.

There is a legend connected with the village. It tells of a young girl who lived here with her mother more than a hundred years ago. One day, a handsome young man drew up outside the house in a carriage pulled by four black horses (today it would be a Porsche). The man stayed in the village awhile, and immediate attraction turned to courtship. In no time at all there was talk of the girl being asked to accompany the man on a journey to the East. Her mother – as usually happens in these cases – was not amused, and sought the advice of the local priest. Armed with his advice the mother returned home to find the man in the living room waiting for the girl to change for the journey. We all know how long a lady can take to make herself look presentable, and perhaps not unwisely the young man had lit a candle giving the girl until it burnt out to get ready. At this, the angry mother blew the candle out and took it upon herself to charge down the road with it to the church. The priest, in his turn, placed the candle in a box and promptly walled it up in a little alcove.

The young man turned out not to be a playboy after all, but the Devil. Realising his secret is out, he flew from the house and drove the carriage off at speed to Affaland Moor, where his reckless driving caused the vehicle to plunge into the bog and disappear in an explosion of blue flame. Thus the girl was saved from a fate worse than death (or a good time, depending on which way you look at it).

Usually Bridgerule is a sleepy little place. It does, however, have two surprising distinctions as far as the Tamar is concerned. First of all, it is the only settlement along the whole of the Tamar's length which sits astride the river, with houses on both banks. Every other village or town touching on the Tamar either sits on the left or the right bank. This fact leads naturally to Bridgerule's second distinction: the village is not, as might be thought, half in Devon and half in Cornwall. Why? Because the villagers refused to be pushed around for the administrative convenience of those in the county halls of Truro and Exeter.

In 1966 the Boundary Commission came to some logical but very ill-advised decisions. Humberside, you may recall, was carved out of Yorkshire; whilst Somerset and Gloucestershire were brutally pillaged for land to create the new county of Avon. All over the British Isles, counties which had remained largely untouched for a thousand years were disfigured and decimated. In consequence, a complete chapter of our heritage was callously cast aside.

Devon and Cornwall did not entirely escape the bureaucrats' arbitrary pencil lines. Many would say, if challenged, that the Tamar is the boundary between Devon and Cornwall. True? Not quite. For as long as the two counties have existed there have been anomalies – areas where the border crept to the east or the west of the Tamar. These were little quirks of history which balked against administrative conformity, and seemed to add a little spice to life on the borders of the two counties.

The Boundary Commissioners decided these anomalies must go. As a consequence, Bridgerule was to be cut in half. Previously, the whole of its parish had been in Devon, part of which extended west of the Tamar. Now the village was to be divided between the two counties, the part to the west of the Tamar would go to Cornwall. The villagers were totally opposed to the idea and decided to fight for the integrity of their community. Meetings were held, protests were made, even a local television camera team was invited to record the villagers' complaints. Finally the Boundary Commissioners relented, deciding that Bridgerule would stay in Devon.

The battle was won by the villagers of Bridgerule, but this skirmish was to prove only the beginning of a protracted war. Throughout the seventies and eighties, there were calls by Cornwall County Council and others to move the boundary to the Tamar. In 1986 the desperate villagers called upon their local M.P. Sir Peter Mills for help. With

Bridgerule village occupies both banks of the Tamar. Here, both are firmly in Devon thanks to the villagers' efforts.

his assistance, another attack was repulsed. The struggle continues.

Fortunately, the Boundary Commissioners saw sense when deciding another boundary issue concerning the boundaries of Devon and Cornwall. In the south of the peninsula Plymouth had launched a campaign to have its own 'Tamarside' county; this would take in an area roughly stretching from Kingsbridge, through Tavistock and Liskeard, to Looe. If the Plymouth councillors had been granted their requests (and it was a close decision) a great swathe of land would have been carved from Devon and Cornwall. The name Tamarside sounds good enough, but the idea seems so silly that I am sure, had it been instituted, the Tamar would have turned back north again and joined the long-lost Torridge, rather than become coat peg for an uneasy alliance of Devon and Cornwall cobbled together for the administrative convenience a few power-hungry politicians in Plymouth.

The Boundary Commissioners must have smarted at their defeat at the hands of the people of Bridgerule; nevertheless, they were to take their revenge on the county. Ten miles south of Bridgerule lies the quiet rural parish of Werrington. From the days when the Saxons arrived in this country it has experienced an interesting history.

In the year 838, as the Saxons were beginning to push the Celts back into what we now know as Cornwall, the parishes were taken over by the royal demesne of Wessex. In 1020 they were bestowed upon Princess Gytha (a woman of Danish birth) following her marriage to Earl Godwin – a man of great power and influence in the reign of King Canute (the one who took an active interest in tidal research). Gytha was an intensely pious woman, while Earl Godwin patently was not. He enjoyed a hobby of land grabbing, and thought nothing of stealing territory from any source, including the church. Gytha was continually put out by this, and on one occasion it seems she even went on hunger strike rather than eat food from an area which had been stolen from a monastery. Things became even worse for Gytha when her eldest son Swein blotted his copy-book by seducing an abbess.

So, when the opportunity arose, after the death of King Harold in 1066, she decided to hand the land to the Abbey at Tavistock. This happened sometime between October 1066 and the capitulation of Exeter to the Normans in 1086. However, William the Conquerer had called a moratorium on shady land deals following his ascent to the throne and this continued until the release of his best seller, the Domesday Book. Thus, Abbot Sihtric of Tavistock was forced to pay the Conquer's successor, William Rufus, an unspecified amount of money to regain the the area officially in 1096. In return, he received the Manor of Werrington and an ivory knife (his receipt perhaps). Werrington was now firmly in Devon hands and remained so.

For almost nine hundred years the county resisted the efforts of the Cornish to take over the land on the west side of the Tamar. In 1894 the Boundary Commission recommended that the area be given to Cornwall, but Parliament firmly rejected the idea. It was stated at the time that 'the boundaries of Wessex are immemorial'. Similarly, a bill to bring the border east to the Tamar was defeated by a committee of the House Of Lords in 1929. In 1966 however, the Boundary Commission got their own way at last and were given leave to hand the area to Cornwall. Thus, the Parish of Werrington was handed to Cornwall after being in Devon for 870 years.

If the Boundary Commission sought to make the Tamar the county boundary for the whole of its length they failed in their objective. Besides Bridgerule, there remain two other anomalies which, for some reason, the Commission seems to have overlooked: as the Tamar flows out of the Lower Tamar Lake it is entirely in Devon; for almost a mile the Cornish boundary retreats a short distance west of the Tamar. Further to the south in the vicinity of North Tamerton the Devon border retreats for a similar distance eastwards. If these anomalies have remained, the question must be asked why, then, was the whole boundary not moved to the Tamar? Or, alternatively, why were the parishes of Werrington and North Petherwin not left as they were? These questions remain unanswered, but perhaps the Boundary Commissioners decided to leave some anomalies of their own in the hope that they would be written about in nine hundred years.

From Bridgerule the Tamar continues its journey southward through gently undulating farmland. One mile south of the village the stream flows past the remnants of a bridge which used to carry the railway from Holsworthy to Bude. This transport system, like the canal, has been consigned to history and lies abandoned, discreetly decaying amidst the fields and the meadows.

When does a stream become a river? Such dividing lines must be largely the subject of conjecture, but it seems to me that somewhere in this area the Tamar comes of age. Already the flow has been increased by the contributions of minor streams like the Derri Water and the Small Brooke. Not long after passing the old railway, the first of the larger tributaries begin to offer up their waters to the main stream. The River Deer, rising in farm land above Holsworthy, is the first to do so. Less than half a mile further south the River Claw – its source deep in a mid-Devon wood – gives up its waters to the swelling Tamar. A little further on and the delightfully named Lana Lake, having flowed through the hamlet of Luffincott, adds its humble contribution.

There are few waterside residents to witness the Tamar's new found maturity. Scattered settlements stand on the hills overlooking the river, their pleasant country churches occasionally punctuating the skyline, but these are little more than hamlets with tiny congregations struggling to keep their churches alive. North Tamerton, Boyton, Werrington, Tetcott, and St. Giles on the Heath all have their

*The River Deer (right) joins with the Tamar. Perhaps this is
the point where the Tamar stream becomes a river.*

crosses to bear. Sadly there are too few people and too many churches.
Each of these country churches has a distinct individual character.
North Tamerton church, for instance, stands starkly alone on the
summit of a hill; its stout granite construction giving an air of rugged
austerity. Tetcott Church, meanwhile, stands snugly with the out-
buildings of the old Tetcott Manor house. Werrington is an oddity
– the church here is of ancient construction, but the rather exuberant
and over enthusiastic Victorians embellished the building with their
own interpretation of decorative pinnacles and architectural after-
thoughts. The overall appearance is ungainly, but somehow endear-
ing.

Luffincott Church has some similarities with Tetcott. There's one
crucial difference, however. Long ago, it was decided that the tiny
population of Luffincott was too small to support the church. It now
lies redundant and decommissioned, but fortunately is kept in good
repair, and is notable for its square Georgian windows.

A public right of way connects Luffincott with Tetcott and pro-

Luffincott Church waits quietly for a renaissance of Christianity

vides a pleasant afternoon stroll close to the Tamar. The owners of the woodland through which the track passes often cut new paths through these plantations and the local O.S. map cannot be relied upon to show the way with accuracy.

Tetcott Manor was home to the Arscott family until 1788. The house passed to the Molesworth family at the death of John Arscott, the last of the family line. He was quite a character in his day, much talked of and appreciated by those who lived along the middle Tamar. He was not a greatly travelled man, in fact he never once left the south-west, living all his days in the mansion. His renown came partly from his great benevolence to the likes of poor children, and to his great aplomb as host. Also, he was known as a man with an all consuming passion for animals. On the one hand, he was a hunter with horse and hounds; but on the other he took pains to collect and care for animals. The most notable of these must have been his tame toad. It lived in the house with him, and at a given signal would jump onto the dining table and take food from its master to the great surprise of assembled guests. Eventually it passed away following a peck by another of John Arscott's animals, a pet raven.

He was a man of many eccentric habits. It was said that he would often go to Holsworthy on Judicial business carrying a bag of fighting cocks. Also, during Sunday services he was occasionally known to throw apples at the vicar (a criticism of lengthy sermons that should perhaps be practised more widely today). His death at the age of seventy was much lamented. So much so that his devoted servant 'Black John' had to be removed by force from his graveside. He made himself a bed by the churchyard wall and was said to have 'sobbed away the rest of his days'.

About four miles south of Luffincott is a place named Druxton where the Bude Canal once terminated. Little remains today, just the outline of an overgrown basin and a few houses. In contrast, the Tamar at this point seems to be gaining strength all the time; just above Druxton the tumbling Tala Water adds its contribution.

Druxton is an important location on the Tamar for another reason. It is the site of an ancient bridge, one of several to be encountered between here and the sea. Upstream, from this point to its source, the Tamar is spanned by a dozen bridges, but all are comparatively modern. The river flows gently and quietly through Druxton; the Tamar can be a capricious river also. When moved to temper she is both forceful and formidable. The principle reason why there are no old bridges between here and the source is because at various times during the past the river has decided to sweep them away. Even along the middle and upper reaches the gradient of the river is not great. When Atlantic storms sweep violently across the exposed high plateau of North Devon and Cornwall the Tamar's tributaries very quickly funnel the waters down into the Tamar's valley. If the rainfall has been sufficiently torrential the river spills out from the confines of its banks and inundates the surrounding countryside. In the past, uprooted trees and other floating debris have often put pay to less stoutly built bridges.

Druxton Bridge has withstood all the Tamar could throw at it since 1520. Its solid construction spans the river with four stout arches rising fourteen feet above the water. Such an ancient bridge must have many a tale to tell about those who travelled over it. Fortunately, one unusual event in the history of Druxton Bridge was written down, –although it concerned the present bridge's predecessor (swept away

The Tamar ambles between tree-lined banks close to Druxton Bridge

in a flood of course).

In Medieval times the Church did much to maintain and enhance the south-west's transport systems. Down the centuries much church money went into the building and maintenance of new bridges on the Tamar.

In 1370 the man in charge of tithing in the Druxton area tried to force the Prior of Launceston into repairing a small bridge across the Tala Water and seems to have accused him of not doing his duty. The Prior appealed to the Sheriff of Devon, who in his turn ordered an inquest to deal with the matter. A jury was duly assembled. The venue for the inquest was chosen as Druxton Bridge itself. The inconvenience to those who wished to pass over it at the time must have been considerable. Certainly, if some wagons had tried to cross the bridge there would have been a problem. The earthy language of the attendant farmers might easily have seen them charged with contempt of court (or bridge).

Nobody knows why such an unsuitable venue was chosen. Perhaps the Prior had favoured it because this was a bridge maintained by the church. In any event the Almighty did not see fit to collapse the bridge beneath the tithing man as he gave his evidence, which might have been an appropriate judgement. In the event, all the witnesses supported the Prior, who was rightly found not guilty of liability concerning the other bridge. Thus unique chapter in Britain's legal history was closed.

Launceston clings to the slopes of Dunheved crowned by the Castle.

4

Launceston: a Crown of Cornwall, and a King of Fish

Many of the great rivers of the world have a capital city sited on their banks. Oft quoted examples are London on the Thames, Cairo on the Nile, and Buenos Aires on the Plate. It would be absurd (you're no doubt thinking) to say that any capital city is on the humble River Tamar. You would be correct of course. The fact is that the Tamar's capital city is not situated on the Tamar at all, it's about a mile from the river on the Cornish side and has the name Launceston.

This capital city stands proudly clustered around its castle guarding the entrance to Cornwall and has claimed for many centuries to be its capital. But surely the capital of Cornwall, you're saying, is Truro. Not according to those who live in Launceston it isn't.To them, Truro is a mere upstart – a concocted capital, only made so by the building of its cathedral, which admittedly looks splendidly medieval, but in reality was erected in the closing years of the nineteenth century. Another claimant to the crown of Cornwall's capital is Bodmin; but according to the people of Launceston its claim is bogus too. Bodmin seems to have become the Cornish capital almost by default when the county's gaol was moved to it from Launceston in the mid-nineteenth century.

Historically, there seems little doubt that Launceston is the capital of Cornwall. In the reign of Ethelred II (979-1016) it was established as a Royal Mint. This does, however, show the Saxon influence over the town, which was perhaps somewhat resented by the indigenous Cornish. It seems that at the time the Saxons looked down upon the Cornish race as inferiors (and who am I to disagree with them!) In the year 909 for instance, the Saxon Bishop of Crediton was given one of the manors adjoining Launceston (Lawhitton). One reason for this gift was said to be 'so that from thence he might every year extirpate their errors.'

Launceston was a good defensive site, in the middle ages the town around it flourished and grew in importance. Together with Trematon Castle, sited on the River Lynher estuary just before its confluence with the Tamar, it was regarded as the gateway to Cornwall. In 1555 the town was referred to as 'The chief town of the Duchy of Cornwall', and soon afterwards was estimated as having a population of two thousand; by far the largest town in Cornwall at the time. For several centuries it was privileged to send, together with the adjoining settlement of Newport, no less than four M.P.s to Parliament (almost as many as were in the Liberal party in the 1950's).

Geographical considerations were eventually to rob Launceston of its status. It was no doubt seen as too close to Devon for comfort. Not for the first time in this book historical factors were brushed aside for geographical convenience; both Bodmin and Truro are far more centrally situated for the administration of the county and the title of capital seems bound to have been handed westwards sooner or later.

Launceston's location was on more than one occasion to put it in the firing line on the national stage of history. Its most turbulent times came during the English Civil War when Parliamentarians fought for the town in an attempt to enter staunchly Royalist Cornwall.

After the reign of King Athelstan the Tamar ceased to be a boundary between Cornwall and England. But for a time in 1643 the Tamar once again became a disputed boundary between opposing forces. Parliamentarians had swept down through Devon, relieved Plymouth, and were poised to cross into Cornwall. Royalist forces were firmly encamped in Launceston, and were ready to attack any Roundhead force which tried to enter the county.

The garrison at Launceston numbered just over 1,200 men commanded by Sir Breville Grenville and Sir Richard Hopton. An opposing force of Roundheads led by Major James Chudleigh with 1,700 men decided to take the town.

They approached from the Lifton area and attacked the Royalist forces holding the Tamar boundary at Polson Bridge. The attack was successful, and not for the first time the Tamar's crystal clear waters were tainted with scarlet ribbons of human blood. The Roundheads swept on towards Launceston town. The Royalists had prepared defensive positions on top of Beacon Hill just outside the town. Here they managed to repulse the attacks which were furiously thrown at them by the Parliamentarians for most of the day. Seeing the battle turn in their favour, and with the additional arrival of reinforcements from the West, the Royalist commanders sent out their mounted troops to perform a pincer movement in an attempt to cut off Polson Bridge from an anticipated Roundhead retreat. However, Roundhead reinforcements arrived in the nick of time, and held off the attempt to retake the bridge. Later in the day, defeated but retiring in good order, the Parliamentarian army was able to withdraw across the bridge into Devon without significant casualties.

Launceston Castle floodlit by night

History says the war was eventually won by the Parliamentarians. In 1646 their forces once again crossed Polson Bridge, this time overwhelming the defences of Launceston and taking the town. A few months later the rest of the Royalist forces in Cornwall were to capitulate, and the Tamar once again became a quiet backwater dividing two tranquil, rural counties.

In the nineteenth century Launceston lost its pre-eminence to towns further west but it remained, and still remains, a town of much charm and dignity. From its precincts have emerged a number of people who have achieved fame in various spheres. In the eighteenth century the town was the birth place of Philip King, the son of a draper. He was a member of the 1796 expedition to establish a colony at Botany Bay in Australia and later went on to become the third governor of Australia. In 1804 he sent out an expedition to explore Van Diemen's Land (now Tasmania). The result was the founding of a town and the discovery of a particular river. The town was named Launceston and the river named the Tamar. So, on the other side of the world, the Tamar has a double with Launceston on its banks. The river reaches the sea along the north coast of Tasmania. A little further along this coast is sited another town with a familiar name – Devonport. This port is sited on the River Mersey. Somehow, I think when it came to choosing names for rivers and towns in Tasmania the pickers got in a twist.

Whilst on the topic of Australia, two other people born beside the Tamar had a hand in its development. In 1790 a Captain John Macarthur from Plymouth arrived in Australia along with his wife Elizabeth, who hailed from Bridgerule. Together they are credited with the introduction of the famous Merino sheep to that land which revolutionised Australian agriculture and without which the country would have long languished as a minor colony.

The name Tamar does not only appear in Tasmania and Britain; there are two other Tamars to be found around the world. One appears in the South American country of Columbia; here the name applies to a tributary of the Magdalena River which flows to the Caribbean Sea. Perhaps this river got its name via Sir Francis Drake, who explored the coastline of Columbia in the sixteenth century.

The second appearance of the name is in an even more unlikely place – in deepest Siberia, close to the border of Mongolia. Here it is not the name of a river but of a small town. This place's connection with our Tamar can probably be discounted as coincidence. It may have the same root as a symphonic work by the Russian composer Balakirev which has the name 'Tamara'. This is a Russian legend, and is apparently unconnected with the River Tamar legend.

In the Launceston area the Tamar was crossed by a positive

plethora of bridges. I say 'was' because in recent years two of these bridges have disappeared. Downstream of Druxton Bridge stands Higher New Bridge. Higher, because there is another 'New Bridge' which, like this one, is actually a rather old bridge, and is further down river near Gunnislake. This particular old Bridge (Higher New Bridge) replaced another even older bridge, which was known a Netherbridge; this is the reason why Higher New Bridge is sometimes known as Netherbridge. This is not a bad thing, as it does prevent the old Bridges known as Higher and Lower New Bridges becoming mixed up. To complicate matters further, Higher New Bridge has recently been replaced by a very new bridge (1984) which now carries the main road from Launceston to Holsworthy. This new Bridge has officially been called 'Netherbridge', which is perhaps rather surprising, because of all the new bridges on the Tamar this is definitely the newest, but is not called 'New Bridge' like the two old bridges – I hope you're not as confused as I am.

Tamar slowly slips seaward beneath the uneven shape
of Higher New Bridge (Netherbridge).

Higher New Bridge is a solidly built granite edifice, contrasting considerably with its new concrete neighbour. It was built in about 1504 by the Abbots of Tavistock, and now stands quietly in retirement; its high humped back making it look rather like a beached whale, in this case stranded by the tide of progress.

A mile or so to the south two other bridges once stood. Both of these were rail bridges, one carrying the Great Western Railway from Plymouth via Lydford to Launceston, the other the main South Western Railway on its long journey from Waterloo via Salisbury, Exeter, and Okehampton to Launceston, Bodmin and Padstow. Until the mid-1960's Polson Bridge was a good place to watch the Atlantic Coast Express as it thundered over the Tamar carrying its cargo of holidaymakers journeying to a rendezvous with clean air and golden beaches.

The railways have gone now: the Atlantic Coast Express is confined to the history books, whilst no railway tracks exist over vast areas of North Devon and Cornwall to the west of Okehampton or to the north of Gunnislake. Holidaymakers invariably proceed westward by car these days. The total domination of the car can be seen a mile and a half down stream from Higher New Bridge. Here, an ungainly concrete and steel monster stands above the Tamar like some petrified praying mantis. This is the recently completed bridge carrying the A30 into Cornwall; but I suppose this new road has served its purpose; Launceston – like Mafeking before it – has been relieved.

The modern A30 bridge is a clinical affair. There is very little to suggest the entry into another land (Cornwall). Moreover, cars speeding down the gradient into Cornwall are hardly likely to notice the Tamar at all, snaking between the trees far below. The bridge is merely the continuation of a dual carriageway. There is no rise and fall as the road crosses the Tamar. In fact, other than a little sign saying River Tamar, there is no other indication to the motorist that he is crossing a river at all. Thus is progress – another natural barrier is circumvented; the journey is easier, the world becomes a smaller place – but something indefinable is lost.

Standing a little way upstream of the new road bridge is Polson Bridge; now curiously quiet since most of its traffic has been taken away. The bridge spans the river with one large central arch and is a Victorian construction of stone and iron.

Polson Bridge has always been of strategic importance as was seen in the Civil War. Linked with this is its title of the most used gateway to Cornwall which, in turn, gives it a unique place in the maintenance of a Cornish identity.

When kings and princes have visited Cornwall their Cornish hosts have always held great store by an acknowledgement from the visitor that he is entering an area which is not entirely English and has a separate identity. As early as the mid-fourteenth century when the Black Prince (first Duke of Cornwall) visited the county, a ceremony was enacted on the bridge in which a grey riding cloak was presented to him, (it cost 3s 4d) which was to be carried around in his sight for the length of his stay in Cornwall. This was a costly exercise for the Cornish, as the Black Prince's prime purpose in visiting was to collect his Feudal Dues. The ceremony continued at various intervals over the centuries, but eventually seems to have been discarded.

Revival came in two stages; in 1909 the future King George V was presented with the grey riding cloak in a ceremony on Polson Bridge upon his arrival in Cornwall. In 1921 the ceremony of the presentation of Feudal Dues was also reinstated and this took place in Launceston. In 1973 Prince Charles continued the custom of the Feudal Dues at a ceremony which took place in Launceston Castle. On this occasion the Mayor of Launceston presented the Prince – according to custom – with 'one hundred shillings and a pound of pepper'(not to be sneezed at). It seems that the ceremony on Polson Bridge did not take place in 1973. This is not really surprising, as the increase in traffic using the bridge in the last fifty years must have been considerable. If the ceremony had been continued perhaps motorists passing the hold-up would have been met by a sign saying: 'The Royal Family Apologise For Any Delay'. In any case, with the building of the new road bridge, perhaps the ceremony will again be reinstated.

As it passes the vicinity of Launceston the Tamar continues to grow in stature. A broad landscape of rich farmland gently undulates like enormous swells on an endless green sea, its crests punctuated by an arbitrary array of hedgerows and sentinel trees. These fertile fields are crossed by new emissaries in search of the Tamar. Almost as if in a rush to see who can first reach the river, tributaries join the Tamar from both Devon and Cornish banks. At Netherbridge the Ottery (or Attery) offers up its waters to its host. The Ottery and tributaries drain a wide area of North Cornwall and, until recently, in its lower course formed the border between Devon and Cornwall where it marked the boundary of both Werrington and North Petherwin Parishes. A little over two miles from its confluence with the Tamar is Yealmbridge – reputed to be the oldest bridge in Cornwall.

Not far after Netherbridge Devon bears the gift of water for the Tamar – this is the River Carey, its source in deepest mid-Devon amongst the brooding trees of Halwill Moor Plantation. Standing next in line, less than a mile downstream, is the River Kensey. It enters the Tamar after a picturesque journey down through Launceston town.

As if in alternation, a Devon river is next to add its contribution – two miles below Polson Bridge is the River Lyd, which rises high amongst the Dartmoor tors. Perhaps this is the most enthusiastic of all rivers to join the Tamar. Enthusiastic, because for much of its course it races down its valley in a helter-skelter rush to meet its host. There is no better example than at Lydford Gorge, a well established beauty spot; here the river puts on a vivid aquatic display of swirling cauldrons, plunging cataracts and a precipitous waterfall.

Lyd is a very small name for a river, but such a name belies its importance. This is one of the Tamar's most important tributaries. Besides its own waters, the Lyd also brings the waters of the rivers Wolf and Thrushel. These rivers drain a large area of central Devon. The Thrushel rises close to Okehampton, whilst the waters of the Wolf have recently been harnessed in the massive lake of Roadford Reservoir.

As the Tamar grows in size, its importance as a fishery is also increased. At Launceston there is an Anglers Association which has use of a six-mile section of the Tamar and its tributaries. Altogether there are around seventy members who fish for salmon and sea trout. There is another angling club based at Gunnislake, but most of the other stretches of the river are in the hands of syndicates, or are privately owned by individuals.

Salmon, the prize catch of the Tamar, make a remarkable journey upstream from the estuary. They battle with the likes of rapids, weirs, and the seemingly insurmountable Weir Head at Gunnislake on a journey upstream to the spawning grounds. Tamar salmon can weigh as much as seventeen to twenty pounds. They return to the Tamar in early spring, but do not spawn until the following autumn.

Remarkably, such salmon are capable of laying up to eight thousand eggs; they are deposited in a pit dug by the salmon where the river bottom is composed of gravel and other easily movable deposits. The fish hatch after about forty-one days in the Tamar and its tributaries. In Scotland, where the weather is less mild, the process can take as long as ninety days. When they emerge from the eggs the young salmon still has a yolk sack attached to it containing food to allow the salmon to survive for up to twenty-four days. From then on, the tiny salmon have to fend for themselves in the river. It is perhaps not surprising then, that of eight thousand eggs laid, only about two fish survive to reach maturity.

Young salmon stay in the Tamar for between two and three years. When they reach the 'smolt' stage, and are about four ounces in weight, they embark upon the epic journey which will take them down the river to the estuary, out through Plymouth Sound, and westwards across the Atlantic to the rich grazing grounds of the Greenland coast.

After a further three years they return to Britain. Miraculously, they are able to recognise the Tamar entrance from all the other south-western estuaries. Once in the river, they are also able to return to the place of their birth. Experts suggest their acute sense of smell triggers some deep memory which enables them to smell their way upstream and leave the main river at the correct junction if they were born in a tributary.

Ray White is the Fisheries Inspector for the whole of the Tamar drainage basin. He told me that the intrepid salmon make their way from the sea to beyond Bridgerule, and to the upper reaches of the major tributaries. Above Bridgerule, however, the stream is small and occasionally becomes polluted with nitrates and other chemicals brought to the river by run-off from the fields. The National Rivers Authority monitors closely for pollutants entering the water course, but Ray White is assisted by only five wardens with a responsibility to cover the hundreds of miles of rivers and streams in the Tamar basin. Ray reckons that he alone covers some 18,000 miles a year whilst patrolling the rivers. Another problem in maintaining salmon stocks has been the building of reservoirs on the Tamar and its tributaries. One effect of this is to stop the free flow of sediment and gravel along the watercourse in times of high river flow. If gravel beds are not regularly restocked with material travelling downstream, the existing beds become depleted, or too compacted for salmon to dig into them to lay their eggs. Some of the watercourse below Tamar Lakes has been lost in this way. Pits which salmon dig to lay their eggs need to be as large as one foot across and ten inches deep, a difficult enough task in the best conditions.

The building of the huge Roadford Reservoir on the River Wolf has caused some depletion of salmon stocks on the Tamar by removing a considerable area of their spawning grounds in the upper reaches of this tributary. There is, however, a fish hatchery on the Tamar at Endsleigh. Here, both salmon and trout are raised from spawn and transported to quiet pools on the upper tributaries in an effort to stabilise the river's stocks.

The recently established National Rivers Authority has a mammoth task on its hands. Devon and Cornwall alone have more than five thousand kilometres of streams and rivers. The most dangerous hazard is pollution from farms and factories along watercourses. The Tamar's geography makes it particularly susceptible to pollution. Unlike rivers such as the Dart and the Exe, whose sources lie in barren moorland, the Tamar's upper course lies in an area of productive agricultural land. The great danger here is from pollutants escaping from farms into the river. Modern farming practices have entailed the adoption of substances which offer a great potential danger to the river should they escape.

One hazard is fuel oil escaping into the river. Almost unbelievably, it takes just one gallon of oil to cover an acre of water; and you can't just spray dispersants or detergents on it as might be done at sea. To do so is to transfer the toxicity from the water surface to the rest of the stream. Oil spills can only be effectively countered by placing booms across the river to collect the oil and then carefully siphoning it off.

Probably the greatest danger to the river comes from silage; this can be more than two thousand times stronger than domestic sewage. When silage finds its way into a watercourse there is an immediate massive increase of bacteria in the water, this in turn removes oxygen from the water causing fish, and most other things which live in the water, to die of suffocation. Sadly, incidents are still increasing. In 1988 for instance, there was a 35% increase in pollution incidents originating from farms on the rivers of the south-west. One of the stated aims of the National Rivers Authority is to 'achieve a continuing improvement in the quality of rivers through control of water pollution.' They have an uphill struggle. At the moment they seem to be understaffed, and do not appear to have the teeth to bite into the problem. Until very recently, fines imposed upon farm polluters have been insufficiently punitive.

Serious incidents, especially upon the vulnerable upper Tamar still continue to threaten salmon stocks. 1990 was not a good year. A major incident on the River Claw in April caused the death of many fish and entailed a major effort by the N.R.A. to aerate the stream's waters using portable air pumping equipment.

A few months later, in July, 25,000 gallons of slurry poured into the Tamar just south of the Lower Tamar Lake. Five miles of the river became seriously polluted prompting a large-scale operation by the N.R.A. in which three thousand fish were removed from the river. This included salmon introduced to recently reinstated gravel beds. Nevertheless, a large number of fish were not removed in time and a three-mile-long slick of cow slurry made its insidious presence felt, creeping along the river by night, killing all in its path. At the time, Martin Weiler, a regional spokesman for the N.R.A. said, 'We spend so much time and effort getting the river into good shape, and one act of carelessness puts all that work at risk.'

It can only be hoped that the perpetrators of such crimes will incur hefty fines. It is a frightening thought that the delicate ecology of large stretches of the river hangs under a death threat from human carelessness. One inadvertently turned-on fuel tap, one spilled container of silage, and life in the Tamar can be extinguished overnight.

*The old mine chimney, converted into a monument,
crowns the summit of Kit Hill.*

5

From Greystone to Kit Hill: a Land of Indulgence

At the confluence of the Lyd, the Tamar occupies a broad and expansive valley. The river continues to flow through this quiet pastoral countryside for another two miles. Approaching Greystone Bridge there is a dramatic change; the gently undulating farmland is suddenly replaced by ranges of lofty hills; by precipitous slopes rising almost shear from the river, and by dense woodland clinging tenaciously to the steep hillsides.

The Tamar begins to twist and turn sharply, as if in a struggle to push its way through to the sea. There are huge meanders at Inny Foot and at Lammerhooe where the river almost turns back upon itself, appearing to regain its strength before another assault upon this intractable landscape.

Geographers call meanders like those on the Tamar 'incised meanders'. They are a symptom of the land through which the Tamar flows being subject to significant uplift. In other words, over a period of millions of years, large areas of the south-west peninsula were being forced upwards; this can be traced to huge land movements which were taking place throughout Europe at the time. Such huge land movements, which also threw up mountain ranges like the Alps, are in their turn created by the movement of continents on enormous continental plates.

The speed at which the land in the south-west peninsula was being forced upwards is very important. As it was, the Tamar was able to continue its previous course by cutting down through the new rock. The Tamar had previously been a sluggish river flowing over flattish terrain, hence the reason why there were so many meanders; these were superimposed upon the new uplifted landscape. Had the uplift of the land been much greater, the Tamar would have turned its course around and would have been forced to flow to the north coast. If this had happened the legend of Tamara would have been very different – she would have been found by the Torridge and not by the Tavy.

At Greystone Bridge, the beginnings of this area of uplifted land can be seen in the steeply wooded valley which provides a superb setting for this, one of the Tamar's most attractive bridges. It has indeed been described as the finest bridge in Devon and Cornwall. The name Greystone is not a descriptive title concerning the materials the bridge was made out of, but rather is an adaptation of the local place name Greston which was probably misread by early map makers as 'Greystone'.

The bridge was built in the time of Henry VI by John Palmer a merchant and local M.P. Most of the money though, seems to have been donated by Thomas Mede, Abbot of Tavistock. To raise money for such an expensive undertaking, the Abbot dispensed indulgences. By this system, sinners (but only rich ones) could purchase a period of time when their sins would be prayed for officially by the monks. Such a gift of money would also, it was believed, hold them in good stead for the afterlife. On 27th December 1439 Bishop Lacy granted an indulgence of forty days to all penitents contributing towards Greystone Bridge. The indulgence system also took care of the maintenance of the bridge after completion. Churchmen waited on the bridge from time to time to charge travellers. For a small monetary consideration they would receive a modest indulgence. There seems to be no record of what action would be taken if an individual refused to cough up.

Greystone Bridge has survived the test of time extremely well. Five hundred and fifty years after completion it stands almost as good as new, and still carries the main road from Tavistock to Launceston (A388). A single concession to the twentieth century and the motor car are the traffic lights at both ends to control the flow of single-line traffic. A visit to the bridge is particularly recommended in autumn when the surrounding deciduous woods provide a decidedly stunning setting on warm sunny days.

Close to the Devon end of the bridge a track leads away to the north. This is a public right of way leading to the hamlet of Bradstone (just over a mile away). The track offers fine vistas of the Tamar close to the bridge as it rises through woodland past a farm where deer

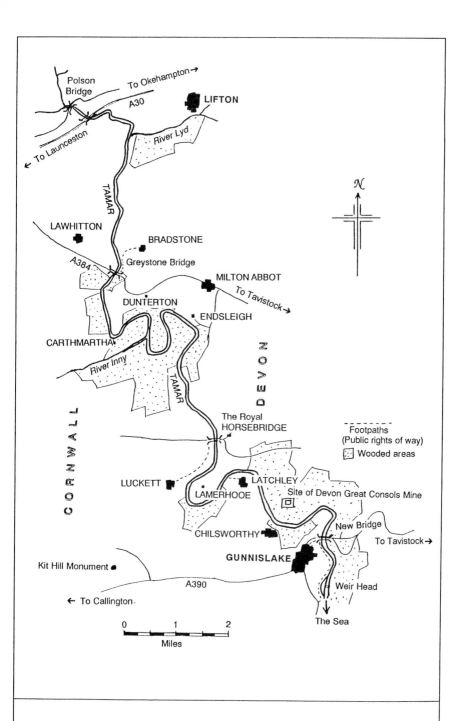

The Middle Tamar

are kept, making a fine sight inside their spacious enclosure.

At the end of the track stands Bradstone Church, which dates from 1261. This church, like several further upstream, has struggled to stay alive. It is little wonder when you consider the surrounding settlement's population is now less than fifty, and was never much greater than a hundred and fifty. To make up for this fact the local residents seem to have made great efforts to compensate for lack of numbers by individual longevity. One particular tombstone, now standing outside the church just to the west of the porch, records:

*Here lyeth the body of John Combe. Buryed the 16th of
Novr being six score years of age, Anno Domini 1604*

The ornate gatehouse at Bradstone Manor

Quite close to the church stands the real gem of the hamlet – the gatehouse of Bradstone Manor. The building is three storeys high, and is topped with a wonderful array of pinnacles and iron work. It is the sort of structure of which any medieval film set would be proud.

From Greystone Bridge the river flows southwards for about a mile and then begins to twist and turn like a writhing snake. In places, the uplift of the surrounding countryside is spectacular, and at one place called Bishops Rock (with no lighthouse) there are spectacular views north and west along the deep tree-lined valley. The viewpoint can be reached from the little village of Rezare (about half a mile away). Although the land here is owned by Tavistock Woodlands, they don't mind too much if people use their track to reach Bishops Rock.

Within sight of Bishops Rock, sited above the river on the Devon bank, lies Dunterton Church, a solitary building with no village in sight. It must take the prize as the most underpopulated of all the settlements along the Tamar. The only sign of a settlement here is a little group of two or three cottages half way down an isolated track some way from the church. In one of the cottages lived Gordon West, a retired journalist who, until recently, dwelt here for many years. He has made an intensive study of the area, and told me that the little church was built in the latter part of the fifteenth century from Green Hurdon stone quarried in Tavistock. The pillar stones of the building, which are made of inferior 'cheesy' granite, were probably cut, he suggests, by a Cornish pagan, and 'have been turning into kaolin since the end of their one year guarantee.'

The lonely little church has not always been so. In archaeological terms Dunterton is a DMV (deserted medieval village). In a field next to the church where there were once houses, no sign of them remains. There is a secret to detecting them. Gordon West told me in a hushed whisper that on some rare autumn days the pattern of the buildings appears as if by magic in the discoloured grass of the isolated field.

How did the village come to be deserted when other villages like Bradstone managed to survive? Gordon dismissed any notion of decimation by plague or gradual decline. He considers it was simply due to rationalisation. The nearby village of Milton Abbot had the facilities to grind barley as well as having its own millers, bakers and stockmen; Dunterton had none of these. Perhaps during a time of poor harvests the villagers decided they had had austerity once too often, and moved *en masse* to the comparative convenience and comfort of Milton Abbot.

Today only the sequestered church remains, standing silently on

Lonely Dunterton Church presides over a landscape of grazing pasture.

the windswept hill. The vicar's flock has been replaced by bleating sheep grazing contentedly in the surrounding meadows.

A little further on from Dunterton the Tamar is joined, almost secretly it seems, by the River Inny. The confluence of the two rivers is hidden deep in woodland far from public roads or pathways. The Inny is an important tributary and can be placed in the 'big four' tributaries to join the Tamar in the fresh water reaches (the Lyd, Carey, and Ottery being the others). The source of the river is high in the mists of Bodmin Moor. Its headwaters, and those of its major tributary the Penpont Water, come rushing down from the moor passing ancient settlements such as Altarnun and St. Clether.

After capturing the prize of the waters from the Inny, the Tamar makes a U-turn towards the north, leaving the wood at Dunterue almost marooned on an island. With an eastward swing, the Tamar finds itself in another land, 'Switzerland'. Well, it looks for all the world like Switzerland. Standing on a slope leading down to the river is a Swiss cottage. It is not alone, but part of a cluster of unusual buildings known as Endsleigh. The main mansion, incongruously named Endsleigh Cottage, was a residence originally built for the Duke of Bedford as a holiday retreat.

The Dukes of Bedford's connection with the area stem from the dissolution of the monasteries. John Russell was appointed by the king to take over lands belonging to the former Abbot of Tavistock. In due course he was ennobled to become the first Duke of Bedford whilst the family's eldest son became the Marquis of Tavistock. The dynasty gained enormous wealth, some of which – as we shall see later – came from local mining. Gordon West asserts they became so affluent that they were able to maintain a house in London's Bloomsbury Square with a staff of more than three hundred servants. It was used for three days a year. Travelling between London and Endsleigh was a ceremonial affair; with the advent of the motor car the Duke's carriage drivers were retrained as chauffeurs. Instead of stopping at livery stables to change horses he would change Rolls Royces.

The house continued to be used by the Russel family until there was an incident when the late Duke of Bedford was shot and killed in the nearby woods. Locals, however, contend that his death was not an accident, but was caused by a self-inflicted wound.

Endsleigh Cottage in an idyllic position overlooking the Tamar.

Today, Endsleigh is a hotel catering for those who can summon up the finance to afford a salmon fishing vacation. The grounds are open to the public on certain days, as is the house where non-residents can acquire an afternoon tea.

The main building was constructed in 1810 by Sir Jeffry Wyatville, and is an outstanding example of what architects call 'The Picturesque Movement', and what laymen might call 'twee'. The estate, however, is extremely well laid out and has superb vistas overlooking the Tamar and its impressive wooded slopes.

In addition to the main house and Swiss Cottage there are other buildings in the grounds which are of interest. There is a 'Shell Grotto' – a sort of summer house covered in a selection of colourful crustaceans; a dairy – an octagonal building surrounded by an open arcade; a Holy Well – a small construction with an inscription stating that it was used as a font by the Abbots of Tavistock, and a row of quaint cottages standing beside a limpid pool.

A huge area extending to some three hundred acres was set aside by the Duke to be landscaped; for this task he hired the services of

Humphrey Repton, a landscape gardener who had laid out such important locations as Russell and Bloomsbury Squares in London. In addition, trackways, or 'rides', were constructed for carriage excursions by the Duke and his friends. It has been said that there are some forty miles of these rides close to the banks of the Tamar.

In fact, the whole area was so carefully set out with everything in the right place that one of the finishing touches was smoke rising from a little house up in the hills. For this purpose a fire was carefully tended in an empty cottage. This extravagant tradition continued until the outbreak of the Second World War, when the Duke presumably did not have a very strong argument in keeping one of his servants from the clutches of the Draught Board.

The hundreds of acres of woodland along this part of the Tamar provide an ideal habitat for various kinds of wild life. Badgers are much in evidence – there is a good population of this pugnacious mammal throughout the countryside skirting the Tamar. Numbers appear to be on the increase – good news for conservationists, but not necessarily for local smallholders who find them almost as much nuisance as the fox population. Most chickens do not sleep soundly in their beds along the Tamar these days.

The wooded areas of the river's banks continue to provide sanctuary for a surprising number of deer. Roe Deer are well established in the Endsleigh area, as are Red Deer. Recently, more than a hundred deer comprising both species were counted in the vicinity of Endsleigh alone. Another more recent introduction of the deer family is the muntjac. These animals were originally native to south-east Asia, but have for some time now been introduced into large parks and estates in Britain. Those which have escaped have adapted well to the British countryside and are increasing in numbers. Muntjacs are easy to distinguish from roes and reds; they are much smaller, growing to a maximum of about two and a half feet tall, and have a very distinctive dog-like bark audible at quite a distance, even in thick undergrowth. Fortunately, the bark is not constantly echoing around the valley; they only resort to it when alarmed.

With Endsleigh behind it, the Tamar again resumes a southward flow. The river passes through two more woods (Gunoak Wood on the Cornish side and Leigh Wood on the Devon) before a much gentler landscape opens out. Gradually the hills reduce in height; a wide verdant valley unfolds, and the rustle of the wind in the tree-tops is replaced by the lowing of prime dairy herds. The Tamar seems to take a well earned rest after its struggles with the uplifted landscape below Greystone Bridge.

In the centre of this broad and restful valley stands Horse Bridge, an almost exact twin of Greystone Bridge. It is not quite as long, but stands out from its surroundings, and is not dwarfed by the surrounding hills. For me, this is one of the most restful places along the entire length of the Tamar. There is a certain air of solitude about the location. Unlike the other impressive medieval bridges of the Tamar, at Greystone and Gunnislake, Horse Bridge is in no hurry. There is no major A-road with the accompanying bustle of east-west traffic. The approach roads to the bridge are winding country lanes; few people choose to cross the Tamar here. The twentieth century seems never to have arrived; time stands still, only the sluggish river glides sedately onward, neatly dividing into furrowed channels beneath the stout stonework of the old bridge.

Being more than five hundred and fifty years old, Horse Bridge is the oldest surviving bridge spanning the Tamar.

Horse Bridge is the oldest surviving bridge across the Tamar, and dates from 1437. It is truly remarkable to consider that the structure is still in mint condition after so many years service. The origin of the name 'Horse Bridge' has been the subject of some conjecture over the years. The most obvious derivation stems from its use by pack horses. Another theory suggests that Horse is really 'Horsa', as in Hengist and Horsa, the two Saxon Warriors who in essence began the Saxon invasion of Britain. It has been suggested that Horsa would have been the inspiration for Saxon attacks upon the Britons in the west country. Certainly a wooden bridge existed on the site before 1437. In fact, when I visited the bridge some years ago I encountered some graffiti on the board which displays the date, and is definitely the most constructive piece of aerosol graffiti I have ever seen. Underneath the inscription 1437 someone had sprayed in bright purple paint, 'No, there was a wooden bridge here in 450' (I think that was the date). One thing is for sure; somewhere in the vicinity of Horse Bridge live the most well educated vandals in the country.

There are few buildings at Horse Bridge; all of these are on the Devon bank. Amongst them is a building which is very important as far as I am concerned – a pub. This is The Royal. Originally, I am told, it was a rest house for nuns (so, not much has changed). With the dissolution of the monasteries it was converted to an inn, and has been so ever since. To begin with it was called The Packhorse, but the name was changed after a visit from Charles I during the Civil War. His royal seal can still be seen engraved in one of the granite entrance steps.

The Royal is a friendly and inviting place, and is very well run by Terry Wood and his son Simon. It needs to be well run; there are very few locals in this tiny hamlet, so people need to be attracted from further afield in order for the place to survive. In this it succeeds admirably, luring regular customers from more than a twenty-five mile radius.

Since the beginning of the 1980's the pub has achieved another distinction – it brews its own beer on the premises, a rarity in these days of mass production. There are three brews on offer in total, one naturally being called 'Tamar', with a specific gravity of 1039. The other brews are 'Horsebridge Best', and 'Heller' (aptly named with a specific gravity of 1060). Terry Wood was also keen to point out that on special occasions – such as Royal weddings – they produce a high quality beer called 'Right Royal Brew' (So come on Edward, get cracking.) The beer is made using traditional processes; there are no short cuts, even the barley is crushed in a mill on the premises.

Every so often the pub is overrun by Cavaliers and Roundheads. It happens when the Sealed Knot Society periodically re-enact famous battles and skirmishes from the Civil War. Horsebridge was another location where Royalists and Parliamentarians clashed in 1644. Royalist forces put up stiff resistance as they tried to check a Roundhead push into Cornwall. However, Parliamentarian forces were eventually to brush them aside at the cost of about fifty casualties on both sides.

The Royal at Horse Bridge.

From the Cornish bank at Horse Bridge a public right of way runs close alongside the river for one mile to the quiet and secluded village of Luckett. To the south of Luckett the land rises to 1000 feet in little over a mile. The rapidly rising slope constitutes the massive northern ramparts of Kit Hill. This huge granite-cored monolith completely dominates Luckett and the surrounding countryside.

The summit affords splendid views in all directions: to the north a landscape of rolling farmland spreads out as far as the eye can see. On sunny days, with good visibility, it is just possible to see the satellite tracking dishes at Morwenstow on the North Cornish coast glinting in the sun. The view from the hill looking south is particularly breathtaking. On clear days most of the Tamar estuary can be seen from the summit, as can Plymouth, and beyond it the Sound, the breakwater, and the impressive Mewstone some seventeen miles distant. The unusual name 'Kit' is a bit of an enigma. The word may have come from the Kittow family who have lived in the vicinity of the hill for many generations. Alternatively, it may be a corruption of the name 'Kite', a bird once native to this part of the world. Also, there is the name 'Fuzz Kite' a Cornish term for the still indigenous buzzard.

If it wasn't for the Tamar and its deeply incised valley, Kit Hill would be part of a finger of high land stretching without interruption between Dartmoor and Bodmin Moor. To me, it seems that Kit Hill belongs to the Tamar. On the approach road not far from the top of the hill, the Tamar can be seen far below, winding through wooded countryside. From the summit itself practically all of the river's domain is within sight, from its beginnings as a hesitant rivulet at Woolley Moor, to its mile-wide estuary merging with Plymouth Sound.

To watch a sunrise at this place is a magical experience. The golden orb appears slowly, breaking free from the dark silhouettes of Dartmoor's highest tors. As it does so the first earthbound rays strike out towards the summits of Bodmin Moor and also to Kit Hill, both becoming bathed in a gentle crimson light. Below in the valley, the Tamar sleeps on, beneath its gossamer blanket of pristine white mist.

The newcomer will have no problem finding his bearings here; helpful plaques, or 'toposcopes' as they are correctly called, have been provided showing the direction and distance of places of interest. These toposcopes stand at the base of Kit Hill monument, a tall tower with a square base and a plinth at its apex, but this not really a monument at all, it is an old mine chimney. When it was built in the last century the Duchy of Cornwall insisted that because it was in such a prominent place it should have a more ornamental design. This 'tarting up procedure' has saved the old stack; all the surrounding mine buildings were demolished years ago.

The chimney has not been the only thing to adorn the summit of Kit Hill. Signs of Bronze age habitation extend far into prehistory. Some stone clusters or 'Barrows' found near the top of the hill date as far back as 3000 years B.C.

Kit Hill also deserves mention in a Civil War context, as do so many locations in this area. In this case a forfeit was built on the summit as a Royalist strong point and look-out. However, once the Parliamentarians had crossed the Tamar bridges, they bypassed this formidable obstacle, leaving the Royalist defences redundant.

There is some evidence to suggest that in the eighteenth century the Hill was topped by a 'Mock Danish Castle'. It could have been built as a folly by John Call, who lived at the mansion of Whiteford near Stoke Climsland, and held the title of High Sheriff of Cornwall (presumably he wanted to be as high as possible).

Next to adorn this high vantage point was a windmill. It was erected in the mid-nineteenth century with the purpose of pumping water out of a mine shaft which had been sunk there for the extraction of tin. Perhaps understandably, this rather flimsy edifice was eventually a victim of the forces it sought to harness, and was blown away in a storm.

In the late 1920's a toll road was constructed to the summit, then adorned by yet another edifice – a cafe. There was also a less intrusive putting green (presumably an over lusty putt would result in the ball rolling down to the Tamar).

At the base of the hill, in the days when mining was at its height, it was decided to drive a tunnel through from north to south – the purpose being to drain water from the mine shafts above. Unfortunately, funds ran out with it only partially completed at either end. In 1959 the tunnels were taken over by the Atomic Energy Authority who drilled five side chambers in the tunnel walls for use in explosive experiments. Rumours quickly spread around the locality that atomic bombs were being tested. It was said that if an accident occurred Kit Hill could be blasted into orbit. In fact, conventional explosives were exclusively used, probably in an effort to discover the relative strengths of rock structures for underground nuclear explosions in other parts of the world.

At the birth of Prince William in 1985 Prince Charles gave Kit Hill to the Cornish (Cornwall County Council). They decided to make the area into a country park accessible at all times to the public. A Ranger was appointed to look after it, and a series of country events were inaugurated to take place on and around the hill. These have included walks, mountain bike races, Bat-Kite workshops, and even open air theatre evenings.

Tamar drifts quietly south beneath the shadow of Kit Hill.

On midsummer eve the crest of the hill is crowned by the glow of firelight. The Old Cornwall Society hold an annual ritual in this sacred place. Prayers of benediction are chanted, herbs are dispensed into the flames, and flags of St. Pirran hang motionlessly in the still night air. Do long departed spirits stir deep within the bowels of the monolith? Does the air thicken with the nebulous presence of Pagan Gods? Are the white robes of resurrected druids seen fleetingly frolicking in the fire light? Who am I to say.

The Tamar's industrial past: an old mine stack hides amongst the undergrowth. The Tamar glimmers beyond.

6

From Lammerhooe to the Tide:
Workings and Woods

Not long after passing beneath Horse Bridge, the Tamar again swings around in a huge meander, this time almost making an island out of the farm at Lammerhooe. On the southern side of the meander are the remains of a ford. A track leads down to it on the Devon side, whilst on the Cornish side a country lane reaches the ford from the compact little village of Latchley. It is a pleasant walk from Latchley to the ford along level ground – a rarity in these parts. The ford is not crossable by motor vehicles even in high summer when the river level is low, but this is a pleasant place to sit beside the river and day-dream.

Lying opposite Latchley are the beginnings of Blanchdown Wood. There are many acres of trees here, but it was not always so. A hundred years ago the woods echoed to the sound of steam engines and pumping machinery. Huge areas of trees were felled and replaced by spoil heaps, waterwheels, and a shanty town of hastily erected buildings and shacks. Blanchdown Wood had been transformed almost overnight from a peaceful reserve for game birds to the largest copper mine in Europe.

This huge enterprise was largely the brainchild of one man, Josiah Hitchins. His greatest achievement seems to have been in persuading the Duke of Bedford, who owned the land, to grant permission for mineral exploration. Had the land Hitchins required been further up-river close to the Duke's 'Cottage' at Endsleigh, there is little doubt the whole enterprise would never have started.

Hitchins quickly set about forming a mining company with the raising of capital via the sale of 1024 shares at £1 each. On 4th November 1844 a rich copper lode was found; it was over forty feet thick in places. Hitchins and his share holders became rich almost overnight; the price of shares rocketed, and not long after were selling at £800 each. The Duke of Bedford was not displeased either; he began to rake in large sums of money in the form of royalties from the sales of copper ore.

As the mine expanded, mine shafts were to proliferate below ground as once trees had flourished above ground. From the shafts radiated thin probing fingers – the levels along which the army of miners toiled, with only the fragile flickering flames of candles to light their way. When the ore was excavated, and brought to the surface, huge voids were left underground; a subterranean world, where cramped clammy passages suddenly opened out into cavernous vaults reminiscent of those of a buried medieval cathedral; but here, there was no sea of stained glass and delicate tracery to let in the light. Total impenetrable blackness dominated. This surely was a malevolent and godless place. The miners stoically went about their work, while their wives as often as not toiled on the surface to break up the copper ore and were known as 'Bal Maidens'. At its peak, the mine – 'Devon Great Consols' – as it became known, employed 1,230 workers and it was calculated that the total swelled to six thousand when those engaged in indirect employment were taken into account.

Steadily, the mine shafts went deeper in search of the increasingly illusive copper ore. There were thirty-five shafts in all; the deepest of these descended to depths in excess of 1,500 feet. To reach the surface, the miners were faced with a climb up unprotected ladders taking about an hour and a quarter. From these shafts, the levels spread out beneath the Tamar itself and into Cornwall. It is estimated that in total these underground levels extended to over forty miles. What an ironic contrast when compared to the Duke of Bedford's carriage drives just a little further upstream, which also extended to forty miles. The comparison of the privileged Duke riding in his carriage, while just around the corner, hundreds of miners toiled below ground, and by their labours helped to line his pocket with royalties, is not a particularly savoury one.

A massive pumping operation had to be mounted in order to keep the lower levels of the mine from flooding. For this, the Tamar itself was pressed into service. Long leats drew off water from the river and carried it to overshot waterwheels placed strategically around the site. These waterwheels, sometimes forty feet in diameter, powered water pumps, and in some cases assisted in hauling the ore up the shafts. Steam power was also used at the mine for pumping. Eventually, steam trains were also used when a railway was constructed to transport the ore to the tidal Tamar at the custom-built port of Morwellham three miles away to the south

Inevitably, the rich copper-bearing lodes were finite; by the 1870's yields were dropping considerably. The mine was able to stay alive, however, by the production of arsenic which was present in many of the copper workings. The arsenic was transported to the southern states of the U.S.A. where it was used to control the 'Boll Weevil' – a moth larva which had a particular liking for the cotton harvest. The product was also used in the production of porcelain, enamel, glass, wallpaper, paint and, perhaps most curiously, by members of the upper classes in various European countries – apparently, when taken in minute quantities, it was said to give the facial complexion a lusty crimson glow (if taken in doses which were over generous, presumably the glow experienced was that of the cremation furnace).

The Tamar heads into mining country near Latchley (looking south).

Arsenic was refined by roasting it in calciners (large ovens) and by a further heating process which resulted in fine white crystals which were nearly a hundred per cent pure arsenic. The arsenic had to be handled with considerable care, especially considering that one-sixth of a teaspoonful was enough to kill a man. The refined arsenic was passed down through leather hoses into paper-lined barrels, and then placed in railway wagons; these were locked upon departure from the mine. It was estimated that from time to time there was enough refined arsenic at Morwellham Quay to kill half the world's population!

Arsenic production could not prolong the mine's life indefinitely. By the time the twentieth century dawned, the company directors knew a reasonable profit could no longer be made from arsenic alone; effectively Devon Great Consols was finished. In 1902 the company was wound up and its assets sold off. Some of the workforce were given jobs on the Duke of Bedford's estate on a temporary basis. Many, though, were to leave the country entirely and headed west to Canada or south to Australia. A few even found themselves with new homes close to the Tamar – but this was the Tasmanian Tamar.

The Duke of Bedford, meanwhile, took no time in raising the mine buildings to the ground in an attempt to restore his woodlands. Unfortunately, some of the remaining spoil heaps were in such a toxic state from the arsenic waste that no vegetation would grow on them. Decades of leaching by rainfall have done little to diminish this, and even today considerable areas remain barren and unproductive.

Trees continue to flourish away from the mine workings. Blanch-down is the first in a succession of woods along the perimeter of the river on the Devon side. From here, stands of trees run almost continuously for three miles to Morwellham and beyond. A good portion of this area is run by the Tavistock Woodland Estate which has done much to foster innovation within forestry circles. The estate was bought by the sixth Earl of Bradford in 1959 who, until his death in 1981 did a great deal to rehabilitate broadleaf trees in the eyes of woodland estate managers. His greatest success, assisted by his chief forester Phil Hutt, was the development of what has become known as the 'Bradford Hutt Continuous Forestry System'. This system seeks to make the most efficient use of space, soil, and light in the production of trees.

The estate grows such impressive varieties as Douglas Fir, Western Hemlock, Western Red Cedar, and Californian Redwood; many of these were introduced to this area some years ago. In fact, near Endsleigh Cottage stands a Douglas Fir which was planted in about 1827. It now stands at a height of over a hundred and fifty feet, and it is estimated that this tree alone contains over one thousand square metres of timber.

Perhaps Tavistock Woodland Estate's greatest claim to fame has come with the recent introduction of a tree known as *Nothofagus Procera* or, more simply, as the southern beech. This broadleaf tree was originally planted in fifteen trial plots. Having originated in Chile and Argentina, it has adapted well to this country. Huge stands of conifers are becoming an all too familiar sight along the Tamar valley and elsewhere. As a cash crop, fast growing firs have been a far better financial proposition for commercial growing. It can only be hoped that the introduction of the Southern Beech and similar species, which are visually more sympathetic to the English landscape, will go some way to redress the balance.

At Blanchdown the Tamar is hemmed in on both banks by encroaching hills. Perched on the Cornish side is the small village of Chilsworthy. The village itself is not particularly picturesque, but there are splendid views to be had along the largely tree-clad valley. Probably the most desirable place to see this view is the village inn The White Hart, but be careful – the inn has been known to sell the strongest commercially available beer in England. It is so strong that the brew is sold in 'Babycham' sized bottles, and has such a full body that it virtually has to be coaxed out with a spoon.

Just around the bend from Chilsworthy is 'New Bridge'; this is the 'Lower New Bridge' and shouldn't be confused with 'Higher New Bridge' near Launceston. New Bridge is the most southerly of the 'Indulgence' Bridges, built at the instigation of the Abbot of Tavistock Abbey. It is a very impressive bridge composed of six arches, each of which stands twenty-three feet above the river. The bridge was completed in 1520, some eighty-three years after Horsebridge. Its completion meant a shorter journey from Tavistock to Callington and Liskeard, and made the bridge at Horsebridge practically redundant. As such, Newbridge must be a rare example of a 'medieval bypass'.

There has been much talk of another bypass in recent years, to

The cathedral-like arches of New Bridge, Gunnislake.

take the very busy A390 away from Gunnislake. Unfortunately, New Bridge is not particularly suited to the motor car. Its roadway is just the wrong size – wide enough to take single line traffic but not quite wide enough to accommodate two lanes. One result is an accident black spot: drivers crossing from the Cornwall side get no sight of the bridge before they are on it. When they do reach it – and if a car is coming from the opposite direction – they suddenly realise there is not enough room for both to pass. The result – wing comes into contact with bridge parapet, an expensive paint job at the very least. The bypass has not yet materialised, even though a strong case was made for it as far back as 1963, when the M.P.s for Tavistock and Bodmin tried to put pressure on the transport department.

New Bridge has encountered many notable figures on their travels. It was, after all, the lowest road crossing point on the Tamar until the suspension bridge was completed at Saltash in the early 1960's. Charles I crossed the bridge in 1644, on his return from the Battle of Lostwithiel. There was also a tussle here between Roundheads and Cavaliers during the Civil War. Essex took the bridge after a 'hot encounter' in which a total of about 240 souls were said to have been lost.

In quieter times the landscape painter Joseph Turner visited the area and stopped to capture a likeness of the bridge. The finished painting is entitled 'crossing the Brook' and depicts two ladies idling away the hours in company of a dog; New Bridge, partly obscured by trees, is downstream in the distance.

A leafy lane follows the river southwards on the Cornish side from New Bridge. This provides a rather pleasant walk with tranquil views of the river in both its fresh water and tidal states. The path eventually turns to join a road ascending into Gunnislake village; from here, the main road completes the circle to New Bridge. Ordnance Survey maps show the precise route, all of which is marked as a public right of way.

Gunnislake is a strange settlement. The name is said to originate from 'Gunnis', meaning an open mine working, and 'Lake', a Cornish term for water. There is, moreover, a lake at Gunnislake, but it is really just an old waterlogged quarry – an ominous looking place with almost jet black water surrounded by practically impenetrable undergrowth. Gunnislake is largely a product of the nineteenth century mining and quarrying boom. It was once a centre of industry. Several companies making bricks surrounded the village; an example of which was the 'Tamar Firebrick and Clay Company' which produced eighty thousand firebricks a week. Other brickmaking companies in the area sent bricks as far away as Russia.

Modern Gunnislake is a somewhat sprawling settlement, practically all of which lies on a steep hill leading up to Hingston Down. The old village centre is bisected by the busy A390, whilst on either side of it more modern developments perch in prominent positions overlooking the river. There is an impressive view from Gunnislake of Hatch Wood on the Devon bank. Here, precipitous crags and rugged scarps tumble almost vertically to the river's edge.

Not far from New Bridge there have been recent developments on the Devon bank. A large pumping station has been built by the South Western Water Authority. The plan is to abstract large quantities of water to augment Plymouth's water supply. Pipes lead away from here, climbing the steep valley sides, then on across the countryside (although buried underground) to treatment works to the north of Plymouth.

In recent years, the Tamar and its tributaries have been used increasingly for the supply of water to a large area of Devon and Cornwall. Upper Tamar Lake, Roadford, and now the scheme at Gunnislake have all been completed in the last twenty years; all have their effect on the environment. Hopefully this pumping scheme will not cause increased silting in the upper tidal reaches of the Tamar. The slow flow on this part of the river already causes a situation during some hot dry summers when oxygen in the river becomes severely diminished, and fish are observed coming to the surface to gasp for air.

The management of our water supplies is not always undertaken in as efficient a manner as might be expected. The contamination in the Camelford treatment works incident, where aluminium sulphate was tipped into drinking water, is a case in point. The proposed construction of a reservoir in the Milton Coombe valley, a tributary of the Tavy, is another example. Here, large amounts of capital were spent to prepare for the construction of a reservoir, new roads were built, and many acres of woodland together with two farms were levelled. It was then decided to shelve the project – and this after millions of pounds had been uselessly spent.

Below Gunnislake the Tamar is a quiet and secluded place. The valley is almost gorge-like on the Devon side, with huge towering rocks rising almost sheer from the river interspersed by areas of foliage where the slope is just sufficient to allow trees to gain a precarious foothold on the rocky terrain. Far beneath, the Tamar, broad and sedate, muses between scattered cottages and wooded banks. Even the tallest trees here are no longer able to stretch out their branches to shade the wide expanse of river from the sun.

The river has grown greatly in stature over the last few miles. Since the confluence of the Inny its flow has been considerable. At Crowford Bridge, not far from the Tamar Lakes, its average flow is 2.5 square metres per second; at Gunnislake, by contrast, it has swelled to 22.4 metres per second.

Half a mile downstream from New Bridge, the Tamar seems to divide around an island. This is no natural island, but the remains of the not too grandly named 'Tamar Manure Navigation'. This is a short canal containing one lock basin. Today, the canal lies unused, its lock gates replaced by concrete barriers. The idea of its builders was not just to bypass the weir at Gunnislake, but to continue the canal northwards to join the Bude Canal, thus creating a navigable waterway right across the peninsula. Unfortunately, this scheme did not even fair as well as that begun by the Bude Canal Company.

Work on the canal was begun around 1798; but only half a mile was ever completed, making the Tamar navigable to barges as far as New Bridge. The enterprise did, however, manage to outlive the Bude Canal – the company remained in existence until well after the First World War. Barges passing through the short canal largely carried manure for surrounding farms, and latterly coal for the gas works at Gunnislake. The canal itself was used as a quayside for the loading of bricks from the nearby brick works at Bealeswood.

Eventually the company folded when coal was no longer brought to the gas works by barge. By 1929 the canal's lock had deteriorated to a condition where it was dangerous. Warning notices were displayed to prevent its use. Liquidation procedures were undertaken as late as 1942; unfortunately, the records of the company were lost in the Blitz on London, and very few details remain of the enterprise. Considering the cargoes carried, this is a story from the Tamar's history that is probably best forgotten anyway.

Tamar near Weir Head.

7
Morwellham and Scenic Grandeur:
the Tamar tastes the Tide

The weir at Gunnislake is probably the most important dividing line on the Tamar. Above it the river's margins are an intimate place; trees line its banks, sometimes merging overhead to shield the river from the sun. Gently rolling hills and meadows characterise much of the upper river's course, whilst below Horse Bridge high and often forested uplands close in on one or both banks. There is little activity. A lone salmon will sometimes silently glide beneath the river's surface sending ripples to disturb the glass like sheen, or the lowing of cattle might disturb the pervasive calm.

The middle and upper reaches of the river are essentially an untouched rural environment; here the river's waters nourish productive fields and meadows, whilst reed bunting and sedge warbler make their nests along its banks. Below Weir Head linnets and goldfinches make way for the habitat of the heron, standing sentinel on the shiny silt beds, and for the sleekly skimming cormorants diving suddenly into the opaque depths of the estuary. Fragile fresh water plants give way to brackish bulrushes, sea lavender and rustling eelgrass. Above all, intimacy gives way to grandeur.

Between Weir Head and the sea the Tamar carries the mantle of a great river with unquestionable majesty. Everywhere there is scenic grandeur; in some places towering cliffs rise shear from the banks, whilst in others the river weaves its way seaward in huge and languorous meanders amidst acres of gently swaying reed beds and the haunting cries of the curlew. If the River Tamar is said to have greatness, then one of its principle claims lies here, where the irresistible forces of the tide transform the river into a paradise for wading birds and sea trout, for gaff-rigged sailing barges, and sedate swans.

The salinity of the water at Weir Head does not change rapidly, there is a slow transformation over about a mile. At first, the water remains dark and clear, but gradually it becomes cloudier and changes to a greenish brown. This muddy colour characterises much of the estuary as far down as Saltash. Visitors confuse this colouration with pollution, but the colour is caused by the stirring up of copious sediment which pervades the river along its estuary. Some locals refer affectionately to the slow-flowing, wide, brown Tamar as 'the great green greasy Limpopo'.

There is nothing more pleasant than spending a lazy hour or so on the river bank watching the sluggish tide rise. Between Calstock and Gunnislake there is often quite a lot of floating debris to be seen on the river. Dislodged reeds, twigs, and branches find their way into the channel and become trapped in these upper reaches in calm weather. The outgoing tide does not take them far enough down river to escape before the next rising tide brings them back again. A couple of hours before high tide will find the flotsam sedately drifting up river like an Armada of Royal Yachts at a naval review.

Weir Head, marking the highest point of navigation on the river and the division between fresh and salt water.

Weir Head is the limit of the tide, and with the closure of the 'Tamar Manure Navigation Canal' is now the limit of navigation for vessels coming up-river from the sea. The river is not just navigable by small boats and dinghies, but is still used by the occasional larger vessel. Several times a year – on the higher spring tides – pleasure boats from Plymouth weave their way ponderously around the sinuous bends of the upper estuary to reach the Weir. Craft of sixty-foot length and a draught of four-feet can reach the highest point of navigation without too much trouble. The biggest problem for skippers making their way along these upper reaches are overhanging trees. In several places wizened oaks or willows lean drunkenly out from the banks, as if the river demanded the shade of parasols of humid summer days.

Many's the time when a passenger on the upper deck of a steamer has had to duck for fear of losing a hat. On occasion I recall a man even had his newspaper snatched away – well, he should have been taking in the scenery. The landscape surrounding the river in this area is truly superb. Less than a quarter of a mile downstream from Weir Head the river turns sharply to the left; all at once a huge wall of rock springs into view like some immense dam stretched across the river.

These are the Morwell Rocks rising shear out of the water to almost four hundred feet. The view from the top is understandably quite breathtaking, especially if a steamer should be passing beneath.

The estuaries of the south-west contain some of the finest scenery in the British Isles. Amongst these estuaries the upper Tamar, to me, reigns supreme; but I'm not alone in this view, there are others who agree with me. The famous pre-war Devon explorer Raymond B. Cattell wrote a book about Devon's estuaries called *Under Sail through South Devon and Dartmoor*. He says of Morwell Rocks: 'The scenery we have now come upon is probably the finest in Devon, combining the Dart at its best with the grandeur of Moorland dimensions and the subtle colouring of the limestone hills of Torbay.'

Morwell Rocks can be reached on foot along a right of way from 'The Rock' – a crossroads where the road descending to Morwellham Quay leaves the road from Tavistock to Bere Alston. From 'The Rock', where there is a green footpath sign, a lane and then a track run westward to Morwell Rocks, a distance of about a mile. Half way along stands Morwell House; this was once the country residence of the Abbots of Tavistock and is an ancient building, some of which

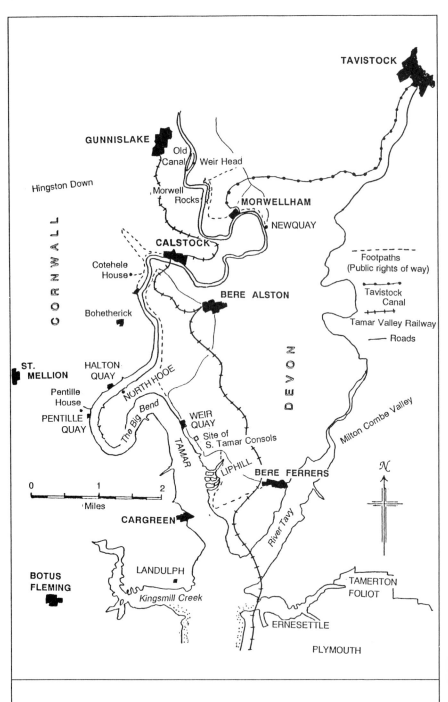

The Upper Tamar Estuary

dates back to the fifteenth century. The Dukes of Bedford were once the owners of the property, but it is now in the hands of the Timpson family.

From Morwell Rocks a path leads down the hill to the River Tamar. From here, another path can be followed in a downstream direction along the river bank to Newquay. Return can be made up the hill following another track bringing you out once more at 'The Rock'. The walk takes about two hours at a gentle stroll, and must be considered one of the most interesting along the Tamar (all these paths are public rights of way).

*The view towards Gunnislake from the summit
of precipitous Morwell Rocks.*

Beneath Morwell Rocks is Impham Turn, here the river bends sharply at an angle of more than ninety degrees. The sudden change in course was the cause of considerable vexation to the skippers of sailing barges. Not only had the bend to be coped with, but also the prospect of baffling winds 'bouncing off' the shear face of Morwell Rocks. Such turbulence could as likely as not blow a barge aground on either bank. Experienced skippers would ensure they had their barge boat (a small rowing boat) ahead to steer them, and the anchor ready to throw, before rounding the bend.

Below Impham Turn the river continues its sinuous course through a mixture of pasture land and high-sided wooded slopes. Overshadowed by one of these slopes lies an island, a very tiny island, measuring just a few metres in length and width, but it splits the Tamar stream in two, and in doing so causes the river to become shallower. Downstream of the island, vessels of up to three hundred tons can navigate the river. The island also has another distinction – it is entirely composed of thick Tamar mud held together by sedge and reeds. When the river floods, part of the island is often washed away; at other times its size is increased when silting takes place. Thus, the island tends to 'move' one way or another. The county boundary at this point follows the middle of the river, so, sometimes the island is in Cornwall, and sometimes it is in Devon. At the time of writing it is mainly in Cornwall, with a little bit in Devon. This surely must be the only island in Britain which can't make up its mind which county (or country) it is in.

Just around the corner from the Island, the scene changes; the left hand bank suddenly opens up to reveal a huge shipping dock; in residence, lying motionless on the mud are sailing barges; there is a railway with ore-filled trucks, and a huge waterwheel cumbrously turning to the hiss of falling water. On the quayside stand gentlemen in black suits with top hats, whilst accompanying ladies wear lace-edged bonnets and carry parasols. It is the nineteenth-century not the twentieth. The Tamar may be a timeless river, but a point is being stretched here.

The Tamar has reached the port of Morwellham on the Devon bank. The nineteenth-century appearance of the place is deliberate; the village and its quaysides have been turned into a museum, dedicated to life and work in the Tamar Valley in the last century; but the history of Morwellham goes back many centuries.

Tavistock lies just over four miles away to the north-east in the valley of the River Tavy. Communications from the town have always been difficult, and one of the easiest routes from the town to the outside world was early on identified as via Morwellham and the Tamar. Tavistock increased in importance in 1305 when it became a stannary town. Morwellham, controlled by the Abbot of Tavistock, very soon became known as 'Tavistock's Port'. Communications however, were not ideal; everything had to be laboriously carried by packhorse. The same problem was experienced by the farmers of central Devon and Cornwall when bringing sand from the coast to improve their soil. The solution was identical – build a canal. Unfortunately, obvious solutions are not always easy to implement. A canal could not be as simply built between Tavistock and Morwellham as was done between Bude and Launceston. It was a matter of geography: between Tavistock and Morwellham stands Morwell Down, a ridge of hills rising to nearly 700 feet, and there really was no way round them.

In 1798 along came John Taylor, an up and coming civil engineer. His suggestion was to drive a canal right through Morwell Down in a tunnel. This was not quite as over-ambitious as it seemed. Along the course of the intended tunnel, it was known that copper deposits existed. Taylor's idea was to exploit the mineral at the same time as the tunnel was being excavated. Mines would be developed using the canal for transport.

Enough people were persuaded to back his idea that in 1803 an Act of Parliament was obtained to start work. His designs were certainly uncompromising. The canal was to have a length of four-and-a-half miles, with one-and-a-half of these inside the tunnel. It would be large enough to carry barges of up to eight tons, and was to have a total drop of four feet, this being just over a foot for each mile of its length.

Work on the bold project began in August 1803. It took seven years to complete the canal from Tavistock to the entrance of the tunnel, but the tunnel itself was to take considerably longer. It was excavated by means of sinking vertical shafts from Morwell Down; from these, the tunnel was bored to the north-east and south-west.

Work was understandably slow. The tunnellers worked with wedges and hand augers tipped with steel. Even so, they often broke, and some can still be found embedded in the sides of the tunnel. Blasting the rock was also possible, but the explosive used for the job, 'Black Rock Powder', was crude and unpredictable. It is perhaps a miracle that nobody was reported killed during the canal's construction. Thirteen years of continuous work on the tunnel saw its completion.

The vegetation-strewn entrance to the Tavistock Canal tunnel above Morwellham.

There were great celebrations on the day when the first barges travelled the canal's length. The opening ceremony was begun as nine barges carrying almost four hundred people came down the canal. They were met by a crowd numbering five thousand at the Morwellham end of the tunnel. Meanwhile, below on the river, berthed vessels fired a twenty-one gun salute.

The final cost of the canal project was £70,000. This sum also entailed the finance for an inclined plane with trucks to lower cargoes to the quayside. Some of the cost of the project was probably offset by the profits of 'Wheal Crebor', a mine which sprang up along the canal's course (as Taylor had predicted).

Nevertheless, this cost was £30,000 above the original budget. As you are no doubt aware, today's civil engineering projects can go wildly over budget – completing the work over the estimate is not just a thing of the past.

With the completion of the canal, Morwellham prospered. Further success for the port followed with the discovery of copper in Blanchdown Woods and the creation of Devon Great Consols Mine. Morwellham was the natural place from which to ship the ore, and it was soon connected to the mine by means of a standard-guage railway and another inclined plane. The quays of the village soon became so crowded that in 1859 some of the riverside houses were swept aside to create a 240 foot dock and accompanying quay space.

In the mid-nineteenth century Morwellham was a thriving place. Ships were constantly departing carrying mineral ores, whilst others arrived bearing cargoes of timber to shore up miles of underground mine workings. Huge waterwheels turned, whilst the clanking of chains echoed across the valley from the busy inclines. Tall masts with acres of furled sails bristled along the quaysides, while sturdy cranes creaked under the weight of their loads. Visitors were amazed; it looked for all the world like a vibrant sea port, but where was the sea? The Tamar, hemmed in by surrounding hills, and still only about sixty feet wide, could hardly be detected zigzagging surreptitiously seaward seemingly in an attempt to remain undetected to the casual gaze.

The fame of this unique port, and of the Tamar Valley itself, grew steadily in the nineteenth century. In 1856 no less a figure than Queen Victoria decided to visit. She arrived at Morwellham on the river steamer *Gypsy* and was met by a guard of honour of 'Bal Maidens' (women who ground and crushed the ores). Her Majesty decided to embark upon an unscheduled excursion to Endsleigh. A messenger warning of the Queen's imminent arrival was sent galloping to tell the Duke of Bedford. The messenger arrived there in the early hours of the morning and, after beating on the door, was greeted with the news that the Duke was not in residence. Upon her arrival, the Queen was shown around by a very surprised and humbled head gardener. Victoria was very taken with the Tamar Valley, and later wrote:

> We... went up the Tamar, which at first seemed flat; but as we proceeded the scenery became quite beautiful — richly wooded hills, the trees growing down into the water, and the river winding so much as to have the effect of a lake.

The decline of Morwellham was inevitably connected to the fortunes of Devon Great Consols Mine. The coming of the railway in its turn was to spell the end for the Tavistock Canal. In 1873 the ailing enterprise was sold back to the Duke of Bedford who for a while continued to make use of it. In 1889, however, records of goods carried on the canal suddenly stop.

Devon Great Consols followed just after 1900. Very quickly, the railway was torn up, the inclines fell to ruins, and the port into profound silence. Gone were the piles of ore, gone were the bustling barges, and gone were the reasons for the little port's existence. Nature began to reclaim the quaysides whilst the timeless Tamar slowly, almost imperceptibly, filled the great dock with a morass of ooze.

The village was not deserted entirely. Some folk stayed on, living in a stout row of cottages built by the Duke of Bedford in the boom years. But many had left the area; in 1908 this forced the closure of the school. The children remaining were taken by cart to the school at Gulworthy two miles away.

The village had declined but the few remaining residents had not lost their will to fight. This was well illustrated by an incident which took place in 1923-24. Miss Ophelia Richards, a teacher at Gulworthy School, had given herself the job of heating the children's pasties at school dinner times. In 1919, however, this practice ceased. The parents of the Morwellham children were incensed that their children were now forced to ride in a draughty school cart in the middle of winter, and have no hot food available for them at school. A council of war at the village decided the children should be withdrawn from school until they could warm their pasties on the premises. A petition was drawn up to highlight the plight of the children but, as is often usual in these cases, the education authorities seemed to be dragging their feet. Eventually, the local M.P., Maxwell Thornton, put the incident onto the national stage by raising the subject in Parliament. Rather swiftly after this, an education sub-committee descended on the school to assess the parents' grievances. The school was promised improved catering facilities immediately – needless to say 'immediately' meant several weeks. It was not long before the old cart was replaced by a charabanc.

The people of Morwellham and their hot pasties passed into memory, whilst their declining village slumbered quietly into obscurity. The great nineteenth-century mining boom may have ended, but Morwellham was made the site of another industry in the 1930's. Many great rivers of the world are renowned for their production of hydroelectricity. A shining example is the 'Aswan' dam on the River Nile which produces hydroelectricity for much of Egypt. The Tamar has a hydro-elecrtric power station too, but it is not in the form of a dam, and neither does it use water from the River Tamar. Water to power the turbines comes from the River Tavy at Tavistock.

In 1933 the West Devon Electric Supply Company hit upon the idea of harnessing the water of the redundant Tavistock Canal to make electricity at Morwellham. A new basin was built above the village and from it a three foot diameter pipe was installed to cover a distance of five hundred feet (not quite vertically) down to the quayside. There, a small building was constructed housing turbines sufficient to produce seven hundred kilowatts of electricity (enough to power seven hundred one bar electric fires at the same time). Of course this isn't quite as much power as created by the Aswan Dam, but Morwellham hydroelectric station remains one of only three in the whole of England, and is second only in production to the station at Mary Tavy, just seven miles away to the north-east.

The used water from Morwellham's power station tumbles out into the Tamar through a wire screen, which prevents inquisitive salmon from swimming up into the mechanism and becoming instant sandwich spread. Thus, the Tamar is swelled by a considerable body of water 'nicked' from the Tavy, some five further up-river from where it should enter the Tamar.

The little power station at Morwellham has been on stream since its completion in 1934. In the 1960's and 70's there was some talk of possibly closing down the station because it didn't produce enough electricity to adequately overcome the maintenance costs of the canal. If the Electrictity Board closed this 'clean' producer of electricity, there is little doubt the environmentalists' lobby would create quite a fuss. With this in mind, they have wisely not taken steps to close the station.

The small staff of the little station remain dedicated to their task, keeping all the machinery in spotless condition. Their devotion to duty went even further in March 1978 when all four walked through heavy snow drifts from their homes in Tavistock to their power station to ensure that supplies were not interrupted at such an important time.

The area of river bank just upstream from the little power station has changed dramatically in the last twenty years. When I first visited Morwellham village it was a quiet, almost deserted backwater. A small cluster of cottages hid amongst the lush undergrowth. There was no shop or pub. Practically all signs of the great port of Morwellham had disappeared. The great docks were filled with reed beds whilst the quaysides, their tiled floors pilfered to build fireplaces, lay deserted, the domain of wild strawberries and wiry bramble bushes. The ochre-coloured Tamar slid silently past old quay walls oozing the sickly sweet odour of rotting wood and wild uncultivated garlic on sultry summer afternoons.

These days things are very different. The old shop and the Ship Inn have been restored; there is a museum, a picnic area, a miniature railway, and even a gypsy encampment. Behind the village is a huge car park, during the season filled with hundreds of vehicles glinting in the sun. Morwellham is now a bustling place where visitors come to see what life was like in the last century; they can even try on authentically recreated costumes from the era.

There is little doubt that the Morwellham Recreation Company have tried hard to create an interesting environment for visitors to enjoy – and have even won prestigious awards for their achievements.

The reclaimed Great Dock at Morwellham at low water. In occupation: the Garlandstone *and a Thames sailing barge.*

In some areas, however, authenticity has been sacrificed. The huge waterwheel turning ponderously at the village centre is not from the Tamar Valley, but from Dartmoor. The mine railway, meanwhile, follows a route where a railway had never existed and enters a mine through an entrance which was specially built for the purpose. Nevertheless, considerable achievements have been made: The Great Dock has been reclaimed from the Tamar mud; in it lies the *Garlandstone*, an original Tamar sailing barge, and another vessel – a Thames sailing barge. A notable (if incongruous) visitor from one great river to another.

On the quayside a sign has been in evidence proclaiming 'No Landing'. Visitors who struggle up the river by boat between shifting mud banks and silty shoals would rightly be indignant to read it. There is no question that Morwellham is the domain of the motor car these days. Gary Emerson, the director of the recreation company, assured me the sign was placed there to, 'deter unauthorised landing at night', but I'm certain this fact is little comfort for those handful of brave boaters who have turned round and gone back down river upon reading it.

What, I wonder, does the River Tamar think of this new recreation empire along its banks? Perhaps the capricious Tamara made her views known in 1979. In that year the Dartington Trust people were rapidly developing the quayside and were building an extensive reconstruction of the railway which brought ores from Devon Great Consols Mine. Huge baulks of timber were being positioned to support the rail tracks ten feet or so from the ground. Following a time of much higher than average rainfall the Tamar suddenly rose up over its banks and totally submerged the quays, carrying with it the standing piles of timber and sweeping away the half-constructed rail sidings. The height of the river during the flood exceeded all others recorded at that location. It is said that the authorities in Devonport Dockyard many miles to the south were forced to make strenuous efforts with an armada of tugs and lighters to shepherd the great logs away from delicate dockside installations. They appeared like a fleet of floating battering rams on the flow of a particularly vicious ebb tide.

The authorities at Morwellham went on to complete the reconstructed railway, and at the moment Tamara is behaving herself, perhaps content that thousands of people each year come to the little port and admire her secluded beauty.

Downstream of Morwellham the Tamar steers a course through a steep-sided but sometimes strangely sinister valley. Here, a century ago, the wonders of nature were bludgeoned into submission. It was a land of hissing steam engines, rumbling water wheels, and belching mine chimneys. Frenetic activity pervaded both sides of the river. Quays and wharfs seemed to occupy every available space along the river's margins, whilst at high tide the river itself played benevolent host to a continuous stream of barges, steam boats, and paddle steamers.

The village of Newquay, situated on the Devon bank half a mile from Morwellham, was a hive of activity a century ago. There were acres of quaysides, a lime kiln complex and a row of quayside cottages. When the mines closed, Newquay died with them. Morwellham managed to remain a small agricultural settlement, but once the mines had gone Newquay had no reason to exist. Within a few years, the place became totally deserted and was reclaimed by the hillside woods. Until recently, no sign of Newquay could be seen from the river. Now, however, things are different. A workforce from Morwellham descended upon the place. Encroaching undergrowth has been cut back to reveal empty shells of houses and the impressive outlines of the lime kilns. Newquay, like Morwellham, has been roused from its slumbers to become a museum piece open to the gaze of the visitor.

Down-river from Newquay, there is profound silence. The old quaysides quietly decompose to the rhythm of the gently rising and falling tide, but nature has struggled to regain predominance. Old mine chimneys stand defiantly beside the river and on the skyline, marking the positions of mines like lofty grave stones. A little way down from Newquay on a high ridge overlooking the river stands 'Gawton Stack'. It has been described as the 'leaning tower of the Tamar' because of a considerable list increasing towards the top. This probably happened when it was built and was due to the mortar drying much more quickly on one side than on the other. Alternatively, a strong westerly gale might actually have moved the top part of the stack as the mortar was drying.

There are other reminders of the once active mines. At Gawton, a huge, unearthly spoil heap towers above the river; it has been estimated that this heap alone contains 124,000 tons of material. The levels of Gawton Mine spread out like the probing roots of a mighty oak. Some went right beneath the river itself, and it was said that the miners could hear the thump of paddle wheels as the steamers ploughed by on the river above. It is also alleged that underground levels from this area were connected to other mines more than a mile away in the Tavy Valley, and that miners from Newquay would use them as a short cut to get to work.

A little further downstream was Rumleigh Brickworks where, until comparatively recently, people would scavenge for discarded bricks amongst the undergrowth. Rumleigh Brickworks was once crowned by a tall stack, but a lightning strike has reduced it to a tottering ruin – its jagged, decapitated summit the home of nesting birds.

On the Cornish bank stands the remains of Okel Tor mine. The chimney remains intact and is surrounded by crumbling ruins and

The crumbling stack at Rumleigh provides a poignant reminder of the Tamar Valley's industrial past.

slowly subsiding spoil heaps. In places like this nature's reclamation battle is most difficult. These spoil heaps continue to contain a small percentage of arsenic waste remaining so toxic that plant life is unable to recolonise the stark and barren wastes. For many years yet this section of the Tamar Valley will continue to be scarred by eerie and hauntingly silent reminders of a vibrantly industrious, but brutally harsh past.

Around the next bend the green lushness returns, and the austere greyness of spoil heaps are forgotten. The Tamar once more flows slowly between banks along which trees dip to the surface of the water like animals come to drink. Waterside whitewashed cottages have their own small quays and gardens running down to the riverside. Tuckermarsh Quay is an ancient place, connected to an agricultural hinterland by a plethora of paths and trackways. For countless centuries farm produce has been brought to tiny quays like Tuckermarsh to await the falling tide and a passage downstream to the markets of Plymouth and Devonport. The wide sweep of Tuckermarsh bend brings the river within sight of a slender and stately viaduct. We have arrived at the Tamar's chief 'up-river port': Calstock.

Calstock viaduct from the woods below Cotehele House.

The little Gunnislake train trundles up the gradient to Bere Alston.

8

Calstock: Boom Town Barges
and a Branch Line

The village of Calstock clings to a steep bank of the Tamar and is an unusual mixture of ancient and modern. The village centres around the steamer quay, a clutter of floating pontoons festooned with old tyres to cushion the arrival of excursion boats. There is a slipway, a rambling old pub called The Tamar and a ubiquitous population of ducks waddling in and out of the river – usually in pursuit of titbits. Behind the quay the old part of the village staggers up the hill in a series of narrow, almost claustrophobic lanes.

Down-river of the main quay, the waterside of Calstock is a place of considerable contrast. There are modern 'executive style houses', – about as in keeping as the tower blocks around St. Paul's – and traditional cottages with gardens running down to the water's edge, and a boatyard with moorings where yachts and motor boats swing silently to the pulse of the dependable tide.

Calstock, the Cornish answer to Morwellham, was also a mining boom town but, unlike Morwellham, it was in a better position to survive the coming of the railways and the decline of the mines. Calstock's history, though, goes back many centuries and includes a mention in the Domesday Book where the manor was called 'Callestoch'. It was both a port and a ferry crossing place, and has always been of great importance to the life of the valley.

Its zenith came and went with the nineteenth century. In 1865 there were no fewer than seventeen mines at work within a radius of five miles, most of which brought their ores to Calstock for shipment. Where today there are gardens and a car park, a hundred years ago there was a line of quays stretching for well over half a mile, continuously occupied by ketches, schooners, barges and steamers.

On the Devon bank was the Brooming shipyard, which was later to achieve fame under the ownership of James Goss. In this tiny yard, elegant Tamar sailing barges were brought into existence. James Goss used traditional building methods passed down over the centuries. His designs were seemingly plucked out of the air; there were no detailed plans, no precise measurements. Vessels were built by rule of thumb, and took shape in the yard as naturally as a baby in the womb. There were no rejects or imperfect models. What Goss saw in this mind's eye appeared in his yard as if by sorcery, and exactly as he had envisaged. Like some majestic symphony, plucked from nowhere by a composer, a Tamar sailing barge would take form and life from a process which seems to us today as little short of miraculous.

The yard continued until the 1920's. Undoubtedly the most famous sailing barge built there was the *Garlandstone*. She was built in the early years of this century, and had a long working life which took her to Southern Ireland, and to the rivers of Germany. She survived the two World Wars including, in 1941, a perilous voyage back from Eire. There was a considerable threat of being dive-bombed, shelled by a U-boat (she would be considered too small to waste torpedoes on) or, ironically, blasted to matchwood by one of the floating mines laid by the admiralty. Fortunately for her skipper, Captain Murdoch, she survived unscathed.

For a while in the 1960's her fate lay in the balance when she lay neglected at Barmouth, but in the nick of time (as happens in all good stories) she was rescued and restored. Finally, she was brought home to the Tamar, and now lies quietly in retirement on the mud of Morwellham's Great Dock.

The Goss shipyard was, towards the end of its life, overshadowed by a great monument to progress – the 117 foot high Calstock viaduct. This wonderfully graceful structure dominates the valley with its twelve lofty arches. Actually, there are thirteen in all, if you include a small arch spanning the main road at Calstock, but to build a bridge with thirteen arches would have been asking for trouble, so officially the viaduct has twelve arches and a bridge.

The viaduct was built to connect the East Cornwall Mineral Railway to the South Western Railway System at Bere Alston. The mineral railway was eventually opened in 1872, after considerable delays, and served as a much needed transport system to carry ores from the mines on Hingston Down, at Kelly Bray, and at Gunnislake. Originally, the railway was designed as a feeder to the port of Calstock with an incline which ran down to the quayside where the ores were loaded onto ships and barges. In 1890, however, the London and South Western Railway opened its prestigious main line from Exeter, through Okehampton, Tavistock and Bere Alston, to Plymouth. It had been an extravagant exercise in railway building, involving the construction of seventy-six bridges between Tavistock and Plymouth alone. One of these was a steel and stone bridge over the estuary of the River Tavy, with seventeen arches spanning more than a third of a mile.

The opportunity of joining the two railways was too good to miss. The completed line would form part of the Southern Railway's tiny local subsidiary, The Plymouth, Devonport and South Western Junction Railway Company, whose name was only slightly shorter than the length of railway they owned.

Work on the viaduct began in 1904. The Tamar (or Tamara), had second thoughts about the project. The ninth pillar was positioned right in the centre of the river; like the others, it needed a foundation in solid rock. Coffer dams were constructed to enable the workers to dig in the centre of the river; but it turned out to be more like excavating a mine shaft than putting in a foundation. Eventually, after much difficulty in keeping out the water, they struck rock a hundred and twenty feet down. The viaduct was therefore not completed on time; the first train to run across it was two years late – a considerable delay, even by British Rail standards.

The finished article is a triumph of 'aesthetic' bridge construction, made all the more so by the fact that it was not built of local granite as might have been expected, but of concrete. Each block for the bridge was individually moulded for its location and trimmed at the edges to make it look like stone; in essence, the bridge was a giant jigsaw (the picture on the box must have been enormous.) The grace of this concrete bridge is outstanding and illustrates the fact that concrete is not a 'hostile' building medium as many think – it is modern architects who should perhaps be regarded as hostile.

Since its completion, the branch line from Bere Alston to Kelly Bray (one mile from Callington) has been quite popular with tourists, but its time of greatest use came in 1941. Nightly raids of German bombers over Plymouth caused an evening exodus of people from the city. Shelter would be taken anywhere it could be found. The 7.05 pm train at Bere Alston was brimmed full with nocturnal refugees whose foremost thoughts were to flee the city until the first light of dawn spelt safety; the return journey was taken with the agonising apprehension of wondering what would meet their eyes on arrival?

The name Dr. Beeching is enough to make any self-respecting rail enthusiast break into a cold sweat. During the 1960's his 'rationalisation' plans brought about the closure of thousands of miles of branch lines. The line from Bere Alston to Kelly Bray was an obvious candidate. Surprisingly, not all of the line was to disappear, only the section from Gunnislake to Kelly Bray was axed.

Dr. Beeching was not all bad. His long list of proposed closures did not include the Exeter and Tavistock to Plymouth main line which he considered should remain open. Though the axe had been spared, British Rail decided of their own accord to close the line. It seems there may have been a plot afoot: this was an old Southern Railway line, and British Rail's Western Region was largely run by old Great Western Railway Staff. It appears they may have deliberately run down traffic on this line in order to make sure of the continued existence of their own lines. If this was their clandestine plan, it succeeded. The line was hacked off in 1968, but not all of it was closed – the section to Bere Alston and Bere Ferrers still had a respectable commuter traffic. B.R. decided (perhaps reluctantly) to keep this section open, thus creating one of the strangest branch lines in the country.

The Gunnislake Line, as it was then known, consists of the old main line from the outskirts of Plymouth and part of the old branch from Bere Alston as far as Gunnislake. When trains reach Bere Alston, the driver is obliged to reverse his train all the way to Gunnislake because there is no way to turn it round in the station designed for connecting trains. Against all the odds, this remarkable remnant of a railway has survived into the nineties. It is an anachronism, but a very charming one. The forty minute run from Plymouth must be considered one of the most scenic in Britain. The little two-carriage train rattles over the huge bridges where once mighty expresses thundered. Everywhere the Tamar is in evidence; sometimes just a few feet away, sometimes far below in the valley playing hide and seek amidst the woods and the reed beds.

Once Bere Alston is passed, the train crawls tentatively down the gradient to Calstock viaduct, and meanderingly makes its way to Gunnislake. The line here is designated a light railway; the driver is obliged to stop at level crossings, look both ways, and proceed if nothing is coming.

The train itself is run almost like a family concern, with railway staff seeming to know all the locals by name. On one occasion I recall the train standing at Bere Ferrers station when an intending lady passenger lost her shoe, which fell underneath the train onto the track as she was boarding. The driver obligingly moved the train further along the platform, while the guard dropped onto the track and retrieved the shoe. He handed it back saying, 'There you are Cinderella'. The lady concerned hurried aboard crimson-faced.

On another occasion a Saturday afternoon train passed through Bere Ferrers station a few minutes early, leaving behind one passenger who arrived on time and was anxious to watch Plymouth Argyle playing at home. He phoned to complain as soon as he realised that the train had gone. A British Rail official apologised profusely, and promptly sent the hapless train driver and his train back out to collect him.

Geography has greatly contributed to the line's survival. Locals use it to circumvent the narrow lanes and traffic jams on the way to Plymouth while, increasingly, tourists are being attracted to the natural splendour of the Tamar. These days, it is known more grandly as the Tamar Valley Line. The location, half in Cornwall and half in Devon, ensures subsidising grants from both. For the moment the spectre of Dr. Beeching seems very far away; locals can sleep comfortably in their beds (except when the first train of the day at 5.30 rattles through and wakes most of them up.)

The Tamar at high tide stands motionless beside Cotehele Quay.
The sailing barge Shamrock *is laid up to the right of picture.*

9
Cotehele and the Unfolding Estuary

Having created the long waterfront at Calstock, the Tamar seems almost to smell the sea again, and turns decisively to the south towards it. From this bend, the thickly wooded Danescombe Valley meanders its way inland towards Hingston Down. It is hard to imagine, standing beside the river here, the spectre of long ships disgorging their warriors on their way to fight the Saxons in the ninth century.

This part of the Tamar has the air of southern climes. To me, there is a definite suggestion of colonial South America, even the Amazon perhaps. At the mouth of the Danescombe Valley stands the Danescombe Valley Hotel, a nineteenth century building encased in verandahs, and looking very much like the British Ambassador's residence in some steamy South American capital. Downstream of the hotel craggy cliffs rise shear from the water, whilst behind it a densely wooded valley often pervaded by bird calls adds to the illusion.

The Danescombe Valley Hotel is the best located hotel along the Tamar's entire course. The vistas from its verandahs are superb, whilst the interior retains all the architectural details of the last century.

The Tamar estuary has many locations along its banks where the builders of large country houses could compliment their architecture with a superb waterside setting. On the Devon bank almost opposite Danescombe stands 'Ward House', a Georgian country mansion. In recent years it has been renamed Chelfam Senior School and is a residential establishment where boys with emotional problems can be coaxed back into society aided by the seclusion of quiet rural surroundings.

Less than a quarter of a mile downstream on the Cornish side is yet another country mansion. This particular example, however, stands sovereign over all other historical houses along the Tamar's length. It is Cotehele House, a splendid medieval residence which has remained almost completely untouched since the sixteenth century. If the Tamar is nature's timeless river, then Cotehele House, in its own modest way, bears the title of man's most timeless creation along its banks.

The house stands high above the river surrounded by gardens and deciduous woodland running down to the water's edge in a series of craggy escarpments. Cotehele House takes its name from Hilaria de Cotehele who acquired it in 1353. The majority of the house was constructed by Richard Edgcumbe in the succeeding century. He led a charmed life, completing the building of Cotehele House after a series of lucky escapes. The first came with an example of Devon/Cornish rivalry: He was long at loggerheads with the Willoughby family, who owned the manor at Bere Ferrers on the Devon bank. Rivalry became so intense that on one occasion the Willoughbys sent a force across the river to dispose of Richard and burn his house down. Fortunately, neither deed was accomplished.

The medieval entrance of Cotehele House.

Later on, Richard supported the revolt against Richard III. In consequence, the King's agent, Sir Henry Trenowth of Bodrugan, was sent to track down and eliminate him. Trenowth was a formidable opponent, having a good background in robbery and deception, and it was not long before he cornered Richard at Cotehele House. A cordon was thrown around the estate, but Richard was able to escape by stealthily creeping out – and slitting the throat of a sentry. Trenowth's men were soon in pursuit as Richard ran down towards the river. Judging that he could not outrun his adversaries, he took off his cap, put some stones in it, and threw it down into the water. The pursuing party arrived very soon afterwards and presumed Richard had jumped into the water and drowned. His escape was completed with a flight to Brittany. There he stayed until Richard III met his end at the Battle of Bosworth.

Upon his return, he constructed a chapel on the spot where he had thrown the cap into the Tamar. The chapel, dedicated to St. George and Thomas a Beckett, is kept open to the public and is excellently maintained in its original condition by the National Trust (you have to take your hat off to them.)

As for the fate of Trenowth, it was his turn to be tracked down by Richard's men. They cornered him at a place still bearing his name on the cliffs near Portmellon in Cornwall. On this occasion it was not just a weighted hat that found its way into the water.

Richard became a man of power and influence in his later years, and was able to extend and enlarge Cotehele House. This process was continued by his son. The buildings, described by Sir John Betjeman as 'the least changed medieval house in Britain', have maintained their unique Tudor appearance because the Edgcumbe family were to move to their new house at Mount Edgcumbe early in the seventeenth century. Since that date, Cotehele remained in the hands of the family for more than three hundred years, but it was not further extended or changed. In 1947 Cotehele became the first country house to be acquired by the National Trust as part payment of death duties. Since then, it has been thrown open to the public together with its beautiful gardens.

On the hill overlooking Cotehele is what looks like a church tower without a church. Closer inspection reveals that it is triangular in plan and appears to have no use at all. Opinions vary about why it was

The folly tower dominating the Tamar Valley above Cotehele House.

built. One theory suggests it was used to receive signals from the high ground above Edgcumbe House (no doubt there was a special semaphore signal to say, 'put the kettle on, the Edgcumbe's are coming'.)

Queen Victoria was not the only monarch to hear about the Tamar's natural beauty and to want to come to see it. Another royal visitor was Charles II, who took to the river at Plymouth and was given a boat trip along the estuary as far as Saltash. Not to be outdone, George III came up the river by barge from Plymouth in 1789; on this occasion Cotehele was reached. Another theory about the Cotehele tower suggests it was constructed in honour of this visit.

Whatever its origins, the tower affords superb views across the valley to Calstock and down-river towards Plymouth. For most of its life it remained a shell, but in recent years the National Trust have thoughtfully provided a spiral staircase to climb to the top.

The tower and Cotehele House can be reached on foot from Calstock station. The distance is about one and a half miles with views of the river along the entire walk. Both Calstock and Cotehele are good starting points for walks. One such begins at Calstock Quay, proceeds westwards along the waterfront to the Danescombe Valley Hotel, then follows the track along the Danescombe Valley to Norris Green. Return is via another track taking you over the remains of the old incline plane and returning you to Calstock Waterfront. The walk can be extended with a detour from the Danescombe Valley Hotel to take in Cotehele House, Richard Edgcumbe's Chapel, and Cotehele Quay (total about four miles).

Cotehele Quay is situated about a mile downstream from Calstock and is owned by the National Trust. Its quayside buildings have been lovingly restored, one of them is now a museum devoted to the Tamar and the vessels plying its waters over the years. A stone's throw from the museum is an example of such a vessel in the flesh. The *Shamrock* – a restored sailing barge – has its own dock here, but she's not just a museum piece. During the summer months, she is regularly shepherded down-river by a little tug. In the lower estuary she lets down her hair and glides free, while little dinghies scurry around her, their crews curious to encounter sailing on the river as it used to be.

Cotehele Quay was a busy place in the last century. It was not just a landing place for Cotehele House: lime burners and salmon fishermen also frequented the place; there were also those who waited to take their produce to Plymouth and Devonport by steamer. With the arrival of steam power, the 'Market Boat' became an institution along the estuary and continued to run well into the twentieth century. It knitted together the small riverside communities down-river of Calstock and in a way was like a slow bus service, with the advantage that there was plenty of room to move around, buy a pasty for your lunch, and have a good yarn with your friends.

For many years the Tamar played host to the paddle steamer; some provided the market boat service, whilst others were employed in excursion work. These grand and stately vessels brought sightseers from Plymouth and further afield to sample for themselves the natural treasures of the Tamar. A sluggish rising tide in mid-summer would see a flotilla of them ponderously nosing their way up-river between the reed beds and the salt marsh. Their arrival was presaged by the sound of hypnotically lapping paddles and the astringent scent of steam.

The excursion habit proved very popular in the Victorian era, especially after Victoria herself (gawd bless 'er) travelled on a Tamar steamer to Morwellham. Paddle steamers of up to one hundred feet feet plied the Tamar, the larger ones having considerable difficulty in turning round at Weir Head.

Fortunately, the entrance to the Tamar Manure Navigation gave a little extra room. Steamer companies were constantly engaged in a battle to outdo each other concerning the speed and comfort of their vessels. One of the most admired paddle steamers was the *Aerial*; her facilities included two spacious saloons complete with seating upholstered with plush velvet 'especially obtained from France'. There were mahogany tables, stewards to serve tea and coffee, and a piano to provide a gentle musical accompaniment to the natural splendours slipping past outside. Such paddle steamers may not have been as large as those on another great river, the Mississippi, but they were probably every bit as luxurious.

By 1910 most of the steamers on the river were owned by two competing companies – The Millbrook Steamboat Company and another company with the rather ungainly title of The Plymouth Piers Pavilion and Saltash Three Towns Steamship Company Limited. In total more than twenty excursion boats were plying the Tamar.

The tradition of river excursions became so well established with the people of Plymouth that the arrival of the railway at Calstock did little to diminish the habit. The First World War, though, had a devastating effect. Most of the paddle steamers were called up for war service. One of the largest steamers, the *Brunel*, was called into service as a hospital ship in far away Mesopotamia (Iraq) – she never returned. Others, like the *Alexandria* and the *Hibernia*, were put to work at Scapa Flow and Rosyth. These two did return in 1918, but were very much the worse for wear.

The excursion habit was re-established in the 1920's, and for a while it proved just as popular, but competition with the motor coach was beginning to sap the flow of passengers. Within the space of a few years there were not enough customers to fill the spacious decks and ample saloons. The paddle steamers were withdrawn one by one and broken up.

It was not all doom and gloom.The Tamar's unique combination of huge naval leviathans along the lower estuary and captivating tranquillity along the upper estuary still attracted visitors. The Millbrook Steamboat Company continued to offer excursions in a small fleet of vessels spearheaded by the *Western Belle*, acquired in 1935. This seventy foot vessel and her sister ships became part of the furniture in the estuary until 1980.

The Millbrooke Company's vessels were well respected on the river for their spotless appearance and the courtesy of their skippers. The Captain of the *Western Belle* was Les Worth, a cheerful ruddy-faced man. Upon arrival at Weir Head, he would skillfully turn the vessel round on her engines in the narrow channel whilst commenting to the passengers over the loud speakers, 'We're on our way back to Plymouth now. The return trip's always quicker – it's down hill all the way.' If he encountered a small dinghy or motor boat on the narrow stretches of the river, his boat would be slowed to reduce the wash and a cheery wave would be seen from the wheelhouse.

In 1980 the skippers of the Millbrooke boats, who were also directors of the company, decided upon retirement. After eighty years of continuous service on the river the company was sold to outside agencies, and its fleet of seven vessels, the oldest of which was the *Devon Belle* built in 1922, was split up. In 1983 the *Western Belle* sadly departed the Tamar for a new career on the River Dart.

The loss of the Millbrook company has created a void in the life of the Tamar which cannot easily be replaced. There are still a number of pleasure boats on the river. In the year of the *Western Belle*'s departure, seventeen vessels were registered for service on the river with a total capacity of three thousand passengers. Sadly, the emphasis of the excursions has changed. Several of the vessels plying the Tamar have now become 'Disco Boats'. These run evening trips to locations such as Calstock; the purpose is not primarily for the passengers to taste the tranquillity of a Tamar twilight, but to dance to loud music accompanied by flashing lights. There is nothing wrong with the principle of the 'Disco Boat', but they might as well take their passengers out to sea for a few hours, rather than disturb the serenity of the river.

There have been occasions when passengers have been landed in Calstock who have been drinking a little too much. Damage has been caused, and the accompanying rowdy behaviour has not been welcomed in the village. For a while, the local authorities in Calstock considered the problem so serious that they sought to prevent excursion boats from landing their passengers in the village at all. Hopefully, the present owners of pleasure boats will see sense and restrict their Disco Boats to the lower estuary and the Sound. The lament for the loss of the Millbrooke Company cuts deeply into those who live beside the river.

The Tamar at Cotehele Quay is dominated on either bank by high hills largely clad in trees. The river still seems an intimate place and very much locked in by the land. On an early September morning the riverside is an atmospheric place. Often a thick river mist hangs low over the estuary muffling sight and sound, creating a miniature insular world where all around – the trees, the buildings, the old boats – are encased with a cold, dewy clamminess.

All at once, around mid-morning, the sun breaks through, dispersing the pristine mist into small isolated clouds clinging to the woods and the shaded places where the sun's rays have not yet penetrated. The river reveals itself to be a sheet of glass, with a host of misty tendrils rising from its surface. Silence is all-pervasive, save perhaps for the distant call of a curlew, or the gurgling of the tide dancing past the old quay on its journey upstream.

Cotehele Quay is one of my favourite places on the river. The carefully restored quay, the thickly wooded slopes, and the *Shamrock*

*The Tamar at Halton Quay; once a busy port, now a quiet backwater.
Its tiny chapel sits on the waterfront.*

quietly swinging on her mooring, blend together to produce a scene
where the hand of man seems almost to coalesce with the hand of
nature. Serenity reigns, everything is as it should be, the world seems
at peace. At Cotehele Quay the river is only about a hundred yards
wide. Gradually as the Tamar continues its southward course, there
is a broadening of both the river and the surrounding valley. The
banks of the river become dominated by a sea of reed beds nodding
in genuflection to the prevailing breeze. As the tide falls the rivers'
margins reveal banks of rich, oozing mud, mingling with the water
where eddies cause spiralling plumes of silt to stream from the banks
when the tidal flow is greatest.

High above the valley on the Devon bank stands the village of
Bere Alston. The influence of Plymouth is apparent here in the form
of new housing estates, giving the village the appearance of a dor-
mitory town. Bere Alston has a long history, much of it connected
to the mining industry which, in this parish, goes back as far as the
thirteenth century when silver and lead were mined.

In considerable contrast to Bere Alston is the little village of Bohetherick on the Cornish bank, where there has been no recent building boom. Building restrictions make sure there is no unsightly development, giving the place an atmosphere of being suspended in time, a fossilised reminder of past centuries. Bere Alston and Bohetherick are extremes. Perhaps both upset the delicate balance essential to rural life. On the one hand Bere Alston has been swamped by development, but houses are available for those who want to buy. On the other hand, Bohetherick is a 'village in aspic' where housing is at a premium, and those which become available are likely to be far too expensive for locals to invest in.

Just over a mile further downstream stands Halton Quay; here the Tamar is already double the width it measured at Cotehele. Halton Quay is dominated by one of the smallest chapels in England (if that is not a contradiction in terms). This little building – roughly the size and shape of a signal box – stands right at the water's edge and bears a dedication to St. Intract and St. Dominicka. Both were Celtic saints of the Dark Ages who are said to have landed here from Ireland and brought Christianity to much of Devon and Cornwall. Probably the best time to find yourself in the vicinity of Halton Quay is on a mid-summer Sunday. In good weather an outside service is sometimes held to the accompaniment of a brass band. On such occasions the owners of North Hooe Farm, on the other side of the river, consider themselves privileged. Reclining in their waterside garden, bathed in the light of a golden evening sun shimmering on the placid face of the Tamar, they experience sonorous music wafting across the river accompanied by the bleating of sheep on nearby pastures.

Most of the farm land in the valley between Cotehele and Halton Quay is given over to arable crops and stock rearing. This was not always the case; until comparatively recently this area, and a great deal of the valley between Calstock and Cargreen, was dominated by market gardening. A boat trip up-river in early summer a few years ago was likely to be characterised by the sickly sweet aroma of strawberries ripening beneath great banks of glinting green house glass and cloches.

The market gardening industry began to flourish when the railway arrived in the nineteenth century. By 1878, a local newspaper, the *Daily Mercury*, was able to report that fifty families were engaged in market

Moored yachts point their noses to the rising tide at Weir Quay.

gardening in the parish of Calstock alone. It was estimated that six hundred tons of strawberries were dispatched annually to London and elsewhere from the Tamar Valley.

The advantageous south-facing slopes of the Tamar Valley were able to produce crops two or three weeks earlier than many other areas in Britain, and therefore commanded higher prices. The steeper slopes were not always easy to move about on; in many cases dung and lime were slid down the fields on sheets of corrugated iron with a rope attached.

Besides strawberries, the Tamar Valley was famed for its cherry orchards and, in particular, the variety called 'Mazzards'. The climate of the valley was well suited to the growth of cherry trees. It was once reported that a cherry tree at Butspill near Calstock had grown to a height of over seventy feet. This produced considerable consternation in agricultural circles as the previous maximum measured height of a tree of the same species was about twenty-five feet. However, it transpired the tree in question had miraculously taken root on the top of a disused mine chimney, and the measured height included

119

that of the chimney. Nevertheless, one cherry tree at Bere Ferrers was credited with producing 100 lb of fruit in one season.

In the last century the fruit growing industry lived cheek by jowl with the mining industry and, surprisingly, did not seem to suffer because of it. The Tamar Valley continued to be an important fruit producer for much of the present century. In 1957 there were estimated to be 850 holdings employing three thousand people on a full-time basis, and up to ten thousand during harvesting. Besides strawberries, tomatoes, lettuce, chrysanthemums, and anemones have also been valuable cash crops.

The noticeable decline of recent years seems largely to have been due to Brussels (not the vegetable, the place). The Common Market has thrown open British markets to cheaper imports from places where warmer climates preclude the possibility of expensive heating bills. The cherry orchards are all but extinct too – rising labour costs have long since made the crop uneconomic. There are a few small orchards left at Botus Fleming, Bere Ferrers, and Bere Alston, but the great profusion of brilliant white blossom which once characterised a Tamar Valley spring is sadly a thing of the past.

Agriculture is an industry of slow yet inexorable change. As one crop increasingly becomes uneconomic another takes its place. On the slopes of the valley, the rearing of beef cattle has become more widespread. Other crops have also appeared: the great blanket of cherry blossom has been replaced during spring by a blanket of yellow. This is the flowering of rape seed, a new arrival (even though the name might suggest it was introduced by the Vikings).

Common Market directives adopted to get rid of food mountains are also bringing about a change in the Tamar landscape. Farmers are being encouraged to take land out of food production – and to plant trees. In many locations along the valley, what look like little fluorescent tube lights are proliferating. In reality they are protective plastic cases for young saplings. For the first time in a thousand years years Tamarside fields are reverting to woodland – not a bad thing in my books.

Another crop which certainly has my approval has been making steady progress along the valley – vine growing. The Tamar already boasts wine bottles proudly bearing its name. The Vineyard at Harewood near Calstock, in the hands of Alec and Edith Mackonochie is now well established, and produces a fruity white English table wine. Another vineyard near Bere Ferrers was established by former mining engineer Roger Harrison. There seems little doubt that others will follow those already established in taking advantage of the Tamar Valley's mild climate and rich soils.

Mount Ararat is within sight of Halton Quay. This is not the place where Noah's Ark is said to have come to rest (that's in the Caucasus Mountains), but a hill which happens to bear the same name. The hill belongs to the estate of nearby Pentille House, another in the long list of mansions built along the Tamar's banks. This particular example was constructed in 1689 by Sir James Tillie and is actually called a 'Castle', although any such resemblance is merely in its crenellated decoration. Sir James Tille was a somewhat eccentric man as is illustrated by instructions he gave to be carried out when he died. He was placed, fully clothed, in a seated position inside a specially built mausoleum on top of Mount Ararat. Later, his body was removed to a more conventional resting place.

About a mile inland of this section of the Tamar lies the village of St. Mellion. Its church tower can be clearly seen from the river. The church also dominates a little valley on its eastern side. In recent years the valley has been transformed into a golf club with an international reputation.

The idea of creating a golf club was the brainchild of Martin and Herman Bond who started out as potato and pig farmers at Tideford. In 1974 they invited the leading golf course architect J. Hamilton Strutt to design an entirely new golf course out of virgin Cornish pasture land. By 1979 the new course had established such a reputation that it was chosen to host The Benson and Hedges International Open, with a field of players from thirty countries.

Next on the scene came Jack Nicklaus (a golfer of some reputation I'm lead to believe). He was asked to design a second course to rival in difficulty and interest any other golf course in Britain. It was a mammoth task involving the movement of some one and a half million cubic metres of material. The completed course is said by many a golfing expert to be a masterpiece. Nicklaus commented; 'I knew it was going to be good, but not this good – St. Mellion is potentially the finest golf course in Europe.' The new course (par 72) was first played on during autumn 1986, but its official opening came in July 1988 when Nicklaus was joined by another golfing legend, Tom Watson, for a challenge match against Britain's Sandy Lyle and Nick Faldo (the British pair won incidentally).

The St. Mellion Golf and Country Club has grown into a sporting complex of considerable size. It now also boasts tennis and squash courts, a swimming pool, sauna, solarium and a three star hotel. If you'd like to go along to play a round of golf perhaps I should warn you that at present prices the green fees for the 'Old Course' are £17, while those for the 'Nicklaus' course are £50 (yes, I said £50).

Pentille Castle and its adjoining quay stand at the apex of the Tamar's most impressive meander. The river here is a confusion of swirls and eddies at spring tides which sweep along the Cornish bank. The Devon bank, meanwhile, is a backwater dominated by reed beds and mud banks. As the river swings towards South Hooe it's all change, with the river clinging closely to the Devon bank, while the Cornish bank is dominated by a huge mudbank fully a quarter of a mile wide at low tide. This area is known locally as the 'Big Bend', and has always been a hazard to the unwary boatman.

At half tide, the channel appears to be wide and deep – as it is further down-river. Newcomers are often tempted to 'cut the corner', but are unaware the water is so shallow. More often than not a sunny summer day will find at least one boat stranded on the mud bank by the quickly falling tide. Occasionally, larger fin-keeled boats are ensnared, and provide a poignant sight lain over on their gunwales like slowly expiring whales.

On one occasion (many years ago I might add) I found myself in a similar predicament. We were chugging down-river in a twenty-two foot motor boat called *Isis*, paying more attention to the magnificent scenery on either bank than to the channel. We were sticking to the middle of the river, but that was not good enough – the channel was well over towards the Devon bank. Suddenly we noticed that the large outboard motor was beginning to make groaning sounds. A glance over the stern revealed great clouds of mud being churned up by the propeller. Unfortunately, the middle reaches of the estuary are so clouded with sediment that you can't see the river bed even if the water over it is one centimetre deep. We turned the boat and headed for the Devon bank, but the rapidly falling tide was reducing the depth of water by the second, and within the space of a few yards we ground to an ignominious halt amidst the whining groans of the motor whose propeller was merely acting as a food-mixer to the mud bank below.

Noticing how fast the tide was falling, our anxiety rose. The motor was useless, but there was still a chance of kedging her off (throwing the anchor from the bow in the direction of deeper water and hauling on the rope, pulling the boat up to the anchor, and repeating the process). We heaved on the rope with all the strength that mild panic could muster, but the mud would not release its prey, and the water was dropping as if from a plug-pulled basin. We were well and truly stranded. Minutes later we were surrounded by a sea of mud with no water to be seen. The next move was to walk to the nearest village and phone home to say we had be delayed by at least twelve hours. We found a phone in Cargreen; but on the walk back to the boat over the mud bank one of my wellies became stuck in a patch of particularly gloppy ooze. I overbalanced and fell flat on my face. Once on board, I found the boat's water tank empty, and was forced to spend the night well caked in mud on the deck. By morning, my appearance could not have been that far removed from a well dried out Egyptian mummy.

We were awakened at about 3.30 in the morning by the sound of the boat refloating on the rising tide. I opened the fore hatch and peered out. Then I suddenly remembered – we had left the anchor in the mud, and in our disgust at not getting the boat off had not bothered to tie the kedging rope to the bow cleat. I made a grab for the end of the rope, but suddenly it wriggled away from me like a snake as the boat refloated and began to drift away on the tide. Before I could get out onto the top deck, the end of the rope trickled over the side.

Still in pitch blackness, we re-anchored the boat with the spare anchor and, leaving one of our number on *Isis*, the other two of us set out in the dinghy with a torch to search for the anchor rope which, being polypropylene, would be floating on the water somewhere. We could not find it. After a while, our colleague on *Isis* decided to up-anchor and move the boat to the safety of deep water. Moments later we heard the familiar groaning sound of the outboard motor. It had not run aground again, but had run over the anchor rope which had wrapped itself around the propeller. We gave up in frustration, and waited for daylight to tackle the problem. Eventually we arrived back at home base in Stonehouse some fifteen hours late.

Having rounded the 'Big Bend', the Tamar broadens into a fine, wide, and deepening estuary. From here to its mouth, this great estuary is never less than a third of a mile wide, and is often more than a mile. For some distance upstream the river has been able to rival many great rivers for scenic grandeur but now, for the first time, the Tamar can compare with other great rivers in terms of sheer size. From this point, the Tamar is host to a wealth of boating activity – firstly of yachts and small craft, and further on to the steel-sided giants of the Navy.

Weir Quay, a tiny village on the Devon bank, is home to a thriving boat yard and a sailing club, whilst out in the river a moored armada of yachts wait patiently for their owners to take them 'walkies'. Just south of Weir Quay is sited the last visual reminder of the Tamar's mining past. Largely overgrown now, the remains of spoil heaps belonging to South Tamar Consols Mine are surmounted by a crumbling stack. In the mid-nineteenth century this silver and lead mine was one of the most prosperous in the area. The end of the mine's life came in 1863 when the Tamar suddenly broke into shafts and levels running beneath it. It was extremely fortunate that the Tamar chose a Sunday to flood the mine; being Sunday, the mine was deserted. Had the disaster happened on a weekday, there is little doubt that all ninety underground workers would have perished. The mine company tried desperately to find a way to bring the mine back into production. Even Brunel's chief engineer, working on the Royal Albert Bridge at the time, could not find a way to effectively repair the breach, and pump out the mine. It was abandoned soon afterwards. Today, its few remains stand as a stark reminder of a disaster that might have been.

As the Tamar estuary continues a southerly course the Devon bank begins to fragment and almost melt away. It is replaced by an inland sea of salt marsh where a profusion of tiny marsh islands are separated by a host of small wriggling channels weaving over the mud banks. To humans the area might seem like a treacherous boggy morass, but to bird life the place is a paradise. This is the ideal habitat for wading birds, offering acres of undisturbed mud flats where juicy morsels wriggle obligingly, ready to be plucked from the ooze.

The mud itself is a veritable wonderland of living organisms. It has been calculated that estuarine mud is some fifty times more productive than the open ocean. It provides a well lubricated home for the ragworm, a voracious predator which will even attack and devour its own species. Great colonies of crabs exist where rocks and seaweed or the footings of quay walls provide cover when the tide recedes. Mussels, which tie themselves together with fibrous tendrils, exist in vast numbers. Their life style is well suited to estuary life where the fast ebb and flow of the tide provides a constant stream of organism-rich soup for them to filter. Mussels, in their turn, provide the staple diet of the oystercatcher which may devour up to a hundred per day.

For the last forty years one of the most treasured birds on the RSPB's list – after all, they use if for their emblem – has been a regular visitor to this area of the Tamar. For a long time this bird, the avocet, was absent entirely from the British Isles. Records show that after 1824 the bird failed to return to the marshes of East Anglia where it had been most prevalent. Suddenly, in 1947, it reappeared near Great Yarmouth, and rapidly began to re-establish itself in areas of salt marsh around the country. Since its first appearance on the Tamar in the winter of 1952/3, when about ten birds were seen, numbers have increased steadily, and now more than eighty birds are known to appear regularly each year. They begin to arrive either in October or November, but the colony does not achieve its maximum number until December.

The avocet is a very distinctive bird, and is easily spotted, even by the untrained eye. Its plumage is grey/black and white in colour, with white predominating on the underside. Most distinctive, though, is the shape of the long thin bill, which unlike any other wading bird points upward towards the tip. The bill is an essential tool for the bird and is used in a side to side motion to sift the mud.

During the winter season small squadrons of avocets can readily be seen bobbing amongst the reed beds on the lower Tamar and Tavy estuaries. The avocets are often accompanied by small squadrons of bird watchers, their binoculared heads bobbing above the hedgerows. Bird watchers gather in flocks too, and can be seen in sizeable colonies aboard pleasure steamers hired for special winter cruises by bird watching organisations. The naturalist Tony Soper frequently migrates here with organised boat-borne parties. He is no stranger to the Tamar, having lived along the banks of the estuary for some years. The lower course of the Tamar is a haven for many other bird species. Swans are in evidence all year round. Their presence, gliding gracefully together 'in line astern' does much to complement the peaceful environment of the Tamar's side creeks. The most popular location for mute swans seems to be St. John's Lake where more than fifty have been counted in early winter. Varieties of ducks on the estuary proliferate in surprisingly large numbers. One species alone – the shelduck – is represented by up to three hundred individuals. Teal, mallard and widgeon are also much in evidence, and usually make their nests in secluded places along the banks.

Another visitor to the estuary, often on passage from high latitudes to North Africa, is the godwit, a member of the snipe family. This is another wading bird with a distinctive long and pointed bill. The name godwit derives from the Saxon words for 'good' and 'creature'. In other words the Saxons considered them good to eat. However, should you try to remove an individual from the estuary to sample the flavour, you are likely to be immediately 'roughed up' by a small army of bird watchers who are likely to appear from nowhere.

In the reaches of the estuary below Saltash, many varieties of sea birds become evident. Herring gulls and other related species can be seen in profusion. Other birds, such as the tern, are often present in significant numbers. Cormorants and shags are almost always present in the estuary. They are usually seen singly or in small groups perched motionless on the huge dockyard mooring buoys. The close proximity of a boat soon sends them awkwardly scurrying along the water's surface in an effort to get airborne. Perhaps surprisingly, cormorants and shags are not merely confined to the lower estuary but can often be seen on the river's margins as far north as Calstock and sometimes beyond.

Other less frequently spotted birds include the auk, which will occasionally visit the Tamar from the Sound in late winter, and also curlew sandpipers, which can sometimes be spotted in Millbrook Lake during the autumn.

Birds of prey are well represented along the Tamar estuary. Places where there are steep, wooded slopes provide an excellent habitat for buzzards and tawny owls. Peregrines also have been seen occasionally soaring effortlessly above the tree-tops. Probably the rarest bird to have been spotted on the Tamar estuary in recent years is the Foster's tern. A lone individual represented only the second time that this species had been seen in Britain.

A public footpath originating near Bere Ferrers station leads down to the salt marsh where avocets have often been sighted at a place called Liphill. From here, the path can be followed along the edge of the estuary until it joins the road to Weir Quay. From the road at nearby Hole's Hole a further public path leads northwards across the neck of the great meander and onwards to Chelfam School (Ward House). Subsequently, the road can be followed to Bere Alston Station. This five mile walk gives a fine flavour of the Tamar's estuary, whilst the vistas both north and south of the high ground above Hole's Hole can only be described as magnificent.

Tamar estuary at Cargreen deep in bird country; unfortunately,none were available on the day so another animal is standing in.

A short way down-river on the Cornish bank stands the village of Cargreen and its waterside inn The Spaniards. This inn, formerly

127

known as the Royal Oak, has become a popular stopping point for the boating fraternity who, at high tide, can leave their vessels alongside the quay. Unfortunately, some of the old quayside walls were rapidly crumbling, and have been replaced by a huge pile of boulders, which frankly makes the place look a mess when viewed from the river. In contrast, old warehouses on the quay have recently been converted to housing, but blend well with the character of the village.

Just around the corner from Cargreen, Tamara is at long last joined by her well orientated suitor, the Tavy. For the last three miles before joining the Tamar, the Tavy opens out into a broad and placid estuary rivalling the Tamar in beauty and wealth of bird life. The low rail bridge at its mouth, coupled with its narrow and winding channel, deter most boats from entering the river, making this the most peaceful of the Tamar estuary's tributaries. Herons, wary of disturbance, are often seen here, as are many other species of waders. Sometimes, when an autumn tide is ebbing, great flotillas of birds can be seen patiently waiting for their dining table to uncover.

The confluence of the River Tavy, the first major tributary since the Inny, transforms the Tamar into a huge and impressive lake. From its margins, two side creeks snake their way inland. On the Devon side is Tamerton Lake — also known as Ernesettle Creek. The word Ernesettle has its origin in the words 'Eagle's Seat', a sure indication that in times past this noble bird included the Tamar Valley within its territory.

At the head of the creek stands Tamerton Foliot, a pleasant village which, in recent times, has been regrettably overrun by the advance of Plymouth, and now lies within the borders of its Empire. Tamerton Foliot's most famous son was one Gilbert Foliot who, in the twelfth century, became Bishop of London, and was a man of great power and influence in his time. He was a long-time rival of another more famous figure, Thomas a Beckett. Both vied for the position of Archbishop of Canterbury. Eventually, following a closely fought contest, Beckett won the post. Had Foliot been created Archbishop, an infamous chapter of English history – Beckett's murder in Canterbury Cathedral – would not have occurred.

Lying directly opposite Tamerton Lake is Kingsmill Lake. It is one of the quietest and most unspoilt of the Tamar's tidal creeks. On its western shore lies Moditonham Quay. There is little activity here;

occasionally a lone fisherman will be seen casting a line into the still waters, or a squadron of swans musing their way upstream. The old quay is a splendid place to while away a balmy summer's afternoon as the sluggish tide seems imperceptibly to immerse the mud banks. The quay can be reached from the peaceful village of Botus Fleming, once the centre of a fruit growing area.

At the entrance of Kingsmill Lake is the hamlet of Landulph. The ancient church here is the last resting place of Theodore Palaeologus; an impressive name for a man of impressive lineage. His renown lies in the fact that he was the last direct descendant of the emperors of Byzantium. The Empire, earlier known as 'The Roman Empire in the East', was centred upon Constantinople which eventually fell to the Turks in the fifteenth century. Paelaeologus lived for many years beside the Tamar in a house opposite Weir Quay and married a local girl with the much more down-to-earth name of Mary Balls. He died in 1636. In 1795, however, his coffin was reopened by some inquisitive local men. The body was well preserved, and described as, 'In stature, much above the common height. [He had] an aquiline nose, and a very white beard.' Another report suggests that his coffin was again opened in 1840. In 1962 the Queen and Prince Philip came to inspect the tomb; at this juncture, however, he was not exhumed especially for the occasion.

Visible from Landulph Church, standing high on a hill on the Devon bank is yet another church, that of St. Budeaux. This modest building has a claim to fame for being the location where another, perhaps slightly more famous man, Sir Francis Drake, was married to Mary Newman. The lady hailed from Saltash, and it is to Saltash where the wide Tamar estuary is next bound. This place marks an end to the luxuriance of the green and verdant Tamar valley. Sailing boats and salt marsh give way to lofty ships of war and sturdy dockyard walls; pervasive placidity surrenders to industrious activity and the brownish-green of the shallow and silty Tamar estuary is swiftly transformed into the crystal sparking blue of a fathomless and formidable firth.

William III's statue stands high above the gatehouse of the victualling yard.

10
From Saltash to the Sea:
Liquor, Leviathans and Legends

A transformation of the Tamar takes place as it reaches Saltash. The wide estuary is all at once constricted by ridges of hills approaching from both the Devon and Cornish banks. As the river forces its way between these two sets of obstacles its width decreases by half – but what it loses in width it gains in depth. At Saltash it seems as if the bottom has dropped out of the river – the mud banks, so prevalent further upstream, have retreated to the river's margins and to the small side creeks. Most of the river is now taken up in a wide and commodious channel, deep enough to moor the Navy's largest leviathans at all states of tide.

Civilisation has replaced seclusion, the sprawling suburbs of Plymouth confront the sprawling suburbs of Saltash. Coming downriver by boat you are soon aware of the constant thrum of traffic high above you crossing the Tamar road bridge. At regular intervals the sound is joined by the guttural tones of an Inter City Express nosing its way across Brunel's grey, imposing masterpiece.

Saltash is an ancient settlement with a much longer history than that of Plymouth and, with the exception of its enormous neighbour, the town is the most well known settlement on the Tamar's banks. The town itself still manages to maintain a strong individual character even though in recent years it has been inundated by housing developments. Being a major crossing point of the Tamar, it has long suffered major inconvenience from the motor car. A bypass of the main street was effected some years ago, but recently even the bypass had to be bypassed, and now the main road into Cornwall passes under most of the town in a tunnel.

For much of its early history Saltash was dominated by Trematon Castle, situated just around the corner beside the River Lynher. This ancient Norman stronghold, second only to Launceston Castle in importance as a gateway to Cornwall, is still in one piece. It has survived the ravages of many conflicts, including the Civil War in which Saltash was taken and retaken by either side no less than eight times. Unlike Launceston Castle, Trematon is still resisting the forces without – and is not generally open to the public.

Saltash prospered under the protection of the manor of Trematon. The protection was certainly needed – as late as 1403 a raid by the French caused considerable devastation to the hamlets further down the estuary. The importance of the town was further enhanced when the right to operate a ferry was granted to its inhabitants in the reign of Edward III. A strong ebb current is always experienced in the narrows at Saltash during spring tides; at such times the work of the ferrymen in rowing people across must have been backbreaking. One notable passenger to cross the ferry in 1724 was Daniel Defoe; he later recorded:

> We passed the Tamar over a ferry at Saltash, the first town we set foot on in Cornwall. The Tamar here is wide, and the ferry boats bad, so that I thought myself well escaped when I got safe on shore.

There seems little doubt that he would not have tried to escape if cast adrift on a desert island.

In the seventeenth and eighteenth century the prosperity of those who resided at Saltash was added to by a little illicit smuggling — or perhaps I should be truthful and say a *lot* of illicit smuggling. Judging by accounts handed down from those days, the place was from time to time positively awash with French brandy. Old ladies, purporting to be shellfish sellers, would ensure they stocked a good supply of foreign liquors to sell to 'trusted customers'. The revenue service was well aware of the trade and seems to have done its best to curtail it. For this purpose a six-oared preventative boat (the rowing version of a speed boat) was kept at Saltash, whilst another enforcement vessel was kept up-river at Cargreen.

The chief problem seems to have been a geographical one. The Tamar above and below Saltash is endowed with an overabundance of little creeks and inlets. It was all too easy for a shallow draught

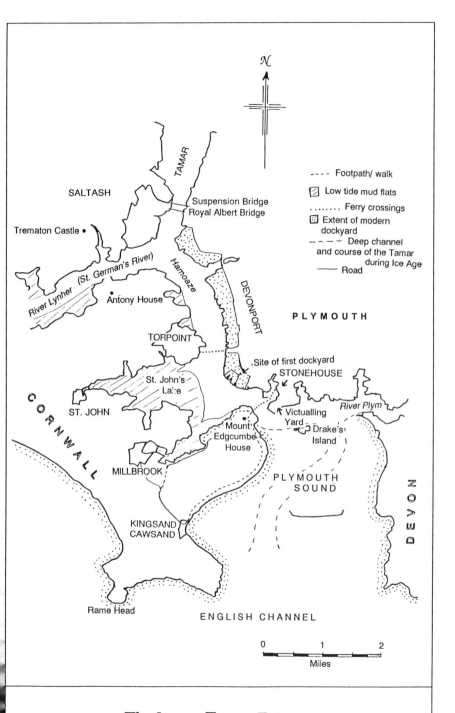

N

---- Footpath/ walk
▨ Low tide mud flats
.... Ferry crossings
⊞ Extent of modern dockyard
– – – – Deep channel and course of the Tamar during Ice Age
—— Road

SALTASH

TAMAR

Suspension Bridge
Royal Albert Bridge

Trematon Castle •

River Lynher (St. German's River)

Hamoaze

DEVONPORT

PLYMOUTH

Antony House

TORPOINT

Site of first dockyard
STONEHOUSE

C O R N W A L L

St. John's Lake

River Plym

ST. JOHN

Victualling Yard

Mount Edgcumbe House

Drake's Island

MILLBROOK

PLYMOUTH SOUND

D E V O N

KINGSAND
CAWSAND

Rame Head

ENGLISH CHANNEL

0   1   2
Miles

The Lower Tamar Estuary

vessel to slip up one of these at night and swiftly unload its cargo without being detected. The large numbers of vessels of all shapes and sizes using the Tamar in those days, coupled with the limited amount of revenue officers, made a regular stop-and-search policy far too expensive.

But the revenue men did have their successes and, again, geographical factors did assist in at least one case. As anyone who sails the lower Tamar will know, the high hills at the Saltash Narrows cause the wind there to play all sorts of tricks. One moment a vessel will be becalmed, while the next minute will see a violent gust appear as if from nowhere. A hapless sailing barge making its way up through Saltash was caught by such a wind, causing her to heel suddenly to port and revealing to all who were standing on Saltash Quay a large number of brandy barrels strapped to the inside of her gunwales. The Customs vessel was soon off in hot pursuit, siren blaring (or at least it would have done if it had been invented).

On another occasion the mere existence of the revenue boats caused the discovery of a cargo of smuggled substances. In this case, the crew of a sailing vessel carrying contraband caught sight of a revenue boat in the river as they passed up through Saltash. Fearing they were about to be boarded and searched, they took their boat further on up-river and ran her aground on the mud at Neil Point near Landulph. All the men abandoned ship leaving the ship's boy in charge. This poor lad valiantly remained at his post, half starved, for three days. Nobody, it transpired, would go out to the boat for fear that the Customs men were keeping a continuous watch on the boat for the return of the crew to remove their illicit cargo.

In the nineteenth century Saltash remained a place of importance, and it was not until well towards the end of the century that Plymouth and Devonport began to overhaul it. The power of Saltash over the trade of the Tamar was considerable and is reflected in the fact that every vessel dropping anchor in the river as far up as Okel Tor (up-river from Calstock) were liable to pay port dues to the burgesses of Saltash.

In 1859, with the building of the Royal Albert rail bridge, Saltash became a railway town The bridge was the wonder of its day and was erected in a unique fashion: each of the two huge central arches were constructed on dry land. When finished, each was floated out

The expansive Tamar above Saltash provides an ideal cruising ground for small boats

on great barges and then raised into position at the rate of six feet per week. Their total height when in position was one hundred feet above sea level. It was insisted upon by the Admiralty who stipulated that the bridge must be high enough for their tallest sailing vessels to sail beneath.

The largest problem in the course of the bridge's construction was the location of the central pillar with a foundation in the deepest part of the river. This presented a similar technical problem to that experienced by the builders of the Calstock viaduct but on a larger scale. The task was eventually completed with the aid of a huge wrought iron cylinder lowered to the river bed. The water was pumped out from it enabling men to descend to the river bed to excavate the foundations.

The completed bridge was a marvel of the Victorian age. Its unique design, incorporating two huge iron tubes to support the railway, has never been duplicated. Today, the bridge still carries the main Penzance line and can bear the weight of the heaviest expresses. A goodly number of the great rivers of the world are spanned by huge and impressive bridges. Many of the modern ones are far longer than Brunel's bridge; but in terms of engineering achievement, longevity, and the shear audaciousness of its builder, the Royal Albert Bridge must stand with the best of them.

The Saltash ferry crossing continued in the shadow of the rail bridge until 1962 when it was superseded by a suspension road bridge – which we are now told is no longer large enough to cope with the volume of traffic. At its time of building the suspension bridge possessed one of the longest unsupported spans in Britain. Since then it has become a minnow in comparison with other bridges like those spanning the Humber and the Severn.

Not far from the Saltash end of the Royal Albert Bridge is a small road leading inland from the foreshore. Standing a little way along it is a small, rather unpretentious cottage. This little dwelling is named after Francis Drake's wife: 'Mary Newman'. She is believed to have lived here for some years before her marriage to Drake. The cottage's fame lies not so much in this fact as in its state of preservation. It has remained structurally intact since that time. There are several large country houses along the Tamar's course which have remained largely untouched for centuries, the most notable of these being Cotehele House, but to find a small 'ordinary' dwelling house in a similar condition is a considerable rarity. Whereas large country mansions have tended to stay in the hands of the same family, who often have wished to keep the buildings in the same condition as their forebears, ordinary small town houses tended to have changed hands on a regular basis. New owners are invariably enthusiastic to make ' improvements' by knocking a wall down here or there, or by adding an extension to the building. All the more remarkable then, that Mary Newman's Cottage has remained in such an untouched state of preservation. Minor changes have occurred to the building over the centuries, but any such 'improvements' were rarely carried out at other than a superficial level, the result being, for instance, that a medieval pre-glass oak window frame was found buried within the masonry of a wall.

Of course it is too much to hope that its furniture has remained untouched over such a long period. The last inhabitant of the house left in 1984; no original Tudor furniture was left by them. No doubt any items of period pieces from M.F.I. or Courts which might have

Mary Newman's Cottage at Saltash.

remained, were considered unsuitable. The Victoria and Albert Museum came to the rescue and have loaned to the building several items of period furniture; not a trace of cheap veneer or chipboard remains.

Who have we to thank for the restoration and preservation of Mary Newman's Cottage? Not English Heritage or The National Trust, as you might have thought, but the Tamar's own conservation organisation – The Tamar Preservation Society. This plucky little organisation was formed a little over twenty years ago, and has been fighting the Tamar's corner with gusto ever since.

The Society burst onto the scene when the old Electricity Board made plans to build a nuclear power station at Insworke Point, a few miles downstream of Saltash. There seems little doubt that such an enterprise, if successful, would have been disastrous, not only from a visual and environmental point of view, but also – with hindsight – from a practical point of view. In the aftermath of Chernobyl the general public will no longer accept the building of nuclear power stations on new sites. The expense of maintenance and of decommissioning has additionally proved such stations undesirable. Fortunately, after the Society made a 'great stink' about the project which was subsequently taken up by the national press, the Electricity Board was forced to abandon its plans. In doing so, it did itself and the Tamar a considerable favour.

The River Lynher joins the Tamar soon after it has passed through Saltash. The confluence of the two rivers provides a superb anchorage where vessels of battleship size can be moored. This area has long been used by the Navy as a place where ships on the 'disposal list' have been moored, awaiting their turn to be towed to the scrapyard. For many years the submarine depot ship *Defiance* was moored here and became very much a part of the geography of the area. Previously, ships of the King George V Class were moored here; they were amongst the last of Britain's battleships, and made a poignant sight moored motionlessly in midstream with great streaks of rust along their sides and huge gun turrets laying silent while awaiting the breaker's torch.

Upstream of the Admiralty moorings the River Lynher provides a stunning contrast with the area around Saltash. It is an unspoilt wilderness, a haven for bird life, and a wide and expansive estuary of great beauty. Three miles upstream the river estuary divides into a series of tributaries. The River Tiddy flows past St. Germans – the site of Cornwall's first cathedral, whilst the Lynher heads away to the north in a deep and often wooded valley, eventually to inhabit the heights of lonely Bodmin Moor.

The River Lynher is a much smaller river than the Tamar. It struggles even to maintain its name on the lower part of its estuary; the alternative name for this estuary is the St. Germans River. The idea of an alternative is infectious; a similar occurrence happens to the Tamar itself once the River Lynher has joined it. The name 'Tamar' appears banished, and the name 'Hamoaze' replaces it from here to the sea.

Hamoaze derives from 'Ham ooze' – the mud of Ham creek which once adjoined Weston Mill Lake. For no logical reason, the use of the word Hamoaze spread from the sixteenth century onwards to take in the whole of the Tamar's lower estuary, but this is still the Tamar – the river does not end at the Lynher's confluence. When the river reaches the sea at Devil's Point it is still firmly known as the 'mouth of the Tamar'. The Hamoaze is merely a convenient epithet to distinguish the lower from the upper estuary, the Tamar does not cease to exist just after Saltash. Geographically too, the Tamar and the Hamoaze are one and the same. The Tamar is the dominant creator of the estuary, with a little help from the ice age, when the river cut a deeper channel to adjust to a lower sea level. The Rivers Tavy and Lynher have had almost no effect on the Tamar's configuration or course. It is not as though the word Hamoaze was used because it was difficult to say whether the Tamar or Lynher had the most important claim to the estuary south of Saltash. Thus, I would contend that the word Hamoaze applies merely as an alternative to the Tamar, and that the Tamar does not end at the Lynher's confluence to be replaced by the Hamoaze.

The southern side of the Tamar and Lynher's confluence remains untouched by modern housing. The banks of the river are still dominated by deciduous trees dipping their branches into the stream at high tide like maidens trailing a hand in a limpid pool.

Tucked away behind the trees, and occasionally seen peeping through them towards the River Lynher is Anthony House. It dates from 1721, and is a superb example of sober and symmetrical Georgian architecture. The house is not large in scale, but its classical plan and proportions make it one of the finest houses in the west country of this period. The inside is elegance itself, and is literally festooned with paintings by Reynolds and furniture by Chippendale. The gardens, like those of Endsleigh Cottage some fourteen miles upstream, were laid out to designs suggested by Repton. The house, now in the hands of the National Trust, can be visited by the public. The surrounding parkland runs down to the Lynher estuary; in late spring this is an enchanting place where a kaleidoscope of colours appears at every turn, and the air is thick with the heady fragrance of countless varieties of luxuriant vegetation. The riverside, meanwhile, provides fine views to the north of Trematon Castle and westwards towards the beauty spot of 'Dandy Hole'.

After Looking Glass Point the character of the Tamar becomes inextricably associated with Devonport Dockyard. From here to the sea, on the Devon bank, the landscape becomes a totally confused and complicated mass of angular quay walls, straggling cranes, ponderous lock gates, burgeoning sheds, peculiar pipes exuding steam, and multifarious warships in various states of undress.

The parkland setting of Georgian Anthony House

Devonport, one of the largest dockyards in Europe, had humble beginnings at Froward Point, about a mile from the Tamar's mouth: William III had landed with an invasion army at Brixham in 1688. The ships that carried his army, being unable to find enough shelter at Brixham, proceeded shortly afterwards to Plymouth. William later visited them, and was no doubt impressed by the great amount of protection afforded to ships in the mouths of the Plym and Tamar. Shortly afterwards he sent down surveyors to begin work.

The establishment of a Dockyard on the Tamar was not an entirely new idea. Since the time of Drake it was thought necessary to spread port facilities evenly around the British coast. In 1625 Charles I had considered plans for a Dockyard at Saltash, but these had been opposed by the locals who did not like the idea of the disruption. The surveyors settled on the idea of building the new dockyard on the Tamar and not the Plym. The decision was reached because the Tamar could accommodate more than a hundred and fifty warships in complete safety. Also, the strong tidal flows in the estuary would act almost like a conveyor belt bringing ships in and out of the estuary when there was not sufficient wind in the right quarter.

In 1692 the first basin and dock were completed at Froward Point; by 1700, the first workman's houses were being built so that dockyard workers did not have to face the long walk to and from Plymouth. This new settlement was called 'Plymouth Dock', and its growth over the next hundred years must be described as little short of spectacular; by 1750 the population was half that of Plymouth, and by about 1770 its numbers had actually surpassed it. The dockyard itself grew at a steady rate along the foreshore transforming the Devon bank of the Tamar. One by one the little creeks and inlets were either filled in or transformed into dock basins whilst the muddy margins of the river were relentlessly dredged and fronted by quays and dock walls.

Meanwhile, the town of Plymouth Dock was becoming restless; its inhabitants balked against the notion of being merely a satellite settlement of Plymouth. In 1824 they declared independence under the new title of Devonport, and began an ambitious scheme of civic building including an imposing Guildhall and a Nelson's column-like monument. Rivalry between the two towns continued right up until the First World War, and was joined by the separate town of Stonehouse sited beside another creek of the Tamar very close to its entrance into Plymouth Sound, but Stonehouse was much smaller than the other two and never really in the race. Eventually, all three grew into one another and were combined as 'The City of Plymouth' in 1914.

The arrival of steam power in the mid-nineteenth century promoted a great deal of activity in the dockyard. New engineering and coaling facilities were created at Keyham opposite the town of Torpoint. Additional basins were also built having a considerable effect upon the Tamarside geography. Keyham Lake, a half-mile long creek ambling inland from the Tamar, disappeared almost overnight.

Ships of the line, their layer-cake broadside batteries giving way to paddle-wheels and iron-clads, in their turn gave way to steel battleships, and in their turn gave way to the *Dreadnought* – a single calibre turret ship making all others obsolete overnight. The Tamar was to witness them all, and the facilities created to cater for them. Such facilities included the 'Great Dock', built in 1895. This huge basin had an area of nearly thirty-six acres.

These later works required a great deal of material, including sand obtained from Start Bay. The acquisition of such sand from the beaches near Hallsands village dangerously reduced its natural sea defences and brought about the village's total destruction during a violent storm at the beginning of the century.

The Dockyard played a valiant role in both of the World Wars. In the Second, it was the target of enemy bombers, but work went on undaunted, even though, every night, trains out of Plymouth – like those to Bere Alston – were crowded with those fleeing from raids.

In total, ten battleships were built on the banks of the Tamar. Amongst their ranks were the *Royal Oak*, the unfortunate victim of a German U-boat attack at Scapa Flow in 1939, and the *Warspite*, arguably the most famous battleship to be built in any British yard in the twentieth century. Her long and distinguished career began at the battle of Jutland and ended when she ran aground in Mounts Bay on the way to the breakers in 1947. Her enviable Second World War record included engagements at Narvik in Norway. In this operation she daringly steamed up an enemy-held fjord and destroyed a flotilla of unwitting German destroyers. Their captains, considering themselves completely safe, had not envisaged the sight of a British battleship steaming up to the protected anchorage.

Devonport Naval base: submarine complex with conventional submarine alongside (right) and nuclear submarine (left).

Following the Second World War the Tamar played host to great aircraft carriers, most notably the *Ark Royal* and the *Eagle*. Towards the end of their lives, when they were part of the reserve fleet, both these monsters were moored in the centre of the Tamar where they became useful windbreaks for those out in boats for a day's fishing. In recent times the sheltered waters of the Tamar have witnessed the age of the nuclear submarine. A base has been created for them at the entrance to another extinguished creek, Weston Mill Lake. Their sinister black hulls are often to be seen sliding ominously along the Hamoaze surrounded by a flotilla of police boat outriders. All private boats are warned to keep well clear; a close approach solicits an angry loudspeakered rebuke. The skyline of the Dockyard is today dominated by the huge frigate refitting complex; these enormous shoe boxes for ships rise to over 160 feet, and are far taller than the deck of the Tamar suspension bridge. Such a massive edifice appears almost like a modern spireless cathedral, a monument to the god of war or, as we like to call it these days, defence.

The river passing the Dockyard is wide, deep, and fast-flowing with both ebbing and flowing tides. Understandably, the thought of falling from a Dockyard wall or being pitched into the river from a boat is not a pleasant one; but such a thought should be accompanied by even greater forebodings. The Tamar has a sinister secret: the legend of Tamara describes her as a beautiful nymph who hated the underworld, and who loved light, air, and sunshine, but Tamara was, after all, the daughter of an earth-goblin. Goblins are mischievous creatures, not averse to wrongdoings. Some of this nature seems to have worn off on Tamara, who, beneath her air of dignity and grace, had a much more ominous side and, although for most of the time the spirit of the River Tamar seems accommodating and benevolent, there is a black side too. This is depicted by another less well known legend which has been fragmented and obscured by the mists of time rather as the surface of the Tamar is often covered by a veil of swirling mist.

The legend suggests the spirit of the river has a malevolent side demanding the sacrifice of a life at least once a year. If a year should pass when there is not a death in or on the Tamar, the river would demand two souls during the next. You may consider such a legend to be mere hocus pocus, but wait to make your judgement until you have heard the evidence.

During the time man has dwelt along the Tamar's banks there have been numerous occasions, no doubt a great many unrecorded, when people have lost their lives in or on the river. The catalogue of unlikely accidents seems to me to take the issue beyond the realms of misfortune or coincidence. For example, the captain of one of the Tamar paddle-steamers was killed whilst lowering his mast to take the vessel under the Tavy railway bridge at the confluence of the Tavy and Tamar. This was a well practised procedure usually offering no significant risk. On this occasion he was unaccountably knocked into the river and drowned. There are many other incidents of accidental drownings: A boy was drowned whilst wheeling a barrow ashore from the schooner *John Simms* moored near Newquay. Another was killed at Weir Head whilst helping to turn a paddle steamer around. In fact, the nineteenth century saw so many drownings in the Tamar that two sheds on the quayside at Calstock served as a mortuary for bodies dragged from the river. Drownings have not just been confined to the tidal stretches of the river – a few years ago a youth was drowned in comparatively shallow water near Horse Bridge. The circumstances of his death were said to be mysterious.

The vast majority of fatalities on the river has occurred on the lower estuary reaches. In 1720 a boat sank at Saltash with the loss of twenty lives. In 1565, the writer Carew records the loss of another boat; all on board were lost with the exception of one woman. In the year 1782 at least five people lost their lives in the Tamar. In July 1701 six women and a man were drowned whilst crossing the river near Cremyll. In 1774 a Mr. Day was lost in the mouth of the river whilst trying out his 'Diving machine' – an early example of a submarine. This was not the only submarine to be lost. Another, 'H29', was lost in mysterious circumstances in 1926. The vessel was afloat in one of the Dockyard basins (filled with water from the Tamar) when she suddenly and unaccountably turned over and sank. There was a desperate attempt to pump out the basin to save those inside, but the operation could not be achieved in time, and six men lost their lives.

In 1940 elements of the French fleet, who had escaped from the advancing Germans, took shelter in in the British ports of Devonport and Portsmouth. It was decided that they should be taken over by the British Navy. The operation went well in Portsmouth, with many thousands of French naval personnel surrendering to the British authorities. Unaccountably, in Devonport, when a British party tried to board the submarine *Surcouf* moored in the Tamar, there was resistance, and four men – two from each side – were shot dead. This incident seems to prove that deaths on the Tamar do not only occur by drowning. This is certainly true of the incident claiming the most fatalities to have occurred on the Tamar's placid waters. In 1796 the frigate *Amphion*, at anchor in the Tamar, was being made ready to sail, and a farewell party was being held on board for the officers and their wives. The commanding officer, Captain Israel Pellow, was in the course of dining with his officers and other guests when a terrific explosion suddenly shook the ship. The captain miraculously survived although the captain of another ship dining with him was instantly crushed by falling wreckage. The ship was totally destroyed with the loss of three hundred lives. Within minutes, only wreckage and the corpses of the crew were left floating on the Tamar's tide. The cause of the tragedy has to this day not been ascertained; it remains one of Tamar's greatest unsolved mysteries.

In the light of the great number of lives lost in the Tamar over the years, there seems little doubt that Richard Edgcumbe knew exactly what he was doing when he declined the idea of jumping into the river at Cotehele. The large numbers of people who have lost their lives on the Tamar seem to prove that the legend must in some part be true. That said, I don't think I'll be dissuaded from spending lazy summer days on board my little boat on the Tamar – but perhaps I will stay a little closer to the bank in future.

Opposite the centre of the Dockyard is the town of Torpoint which has arisen largely in response to the port's needs for manpower. The town is connected to Devonport by three large car ferries running on chains. Even so, there are often long queues of cars waiting to cross the river during rush hours.

The ferry was originally established in 1791. In those days passengers were charged 1d. In recent years there has been a price reduction for passengers, who now pay nothing. In early days the ferry charged five shillings for a coach with four horses. Cars today pay around 40p (eight shillings) to cross – not an enormous increase over two hundred years.

In 1829 the first steam ferry was introduced to the crossing. The

145

One of three Torpoint ferries approaches Torpoint.

vessel was called *Jemima* but she proved unequal to the task, and was frequently washed down-river by strong ebb tides. The strength of the tide was largely overcome in 1834 when chains were laid across the river to hold the ferry on course.

Since its inception the ferry has crossed an exceedingly busy waterway, and there has often been friction between the operators and other river traffic who consider the ferry a nuisance. One incident is recorded when a Naval brig stood in the way of the ferry; a shot was fired from a musket through the hat of a 'much alarmed' passenger. A prosecution resulted.

Today, with three ferries crossing the river within yards of each other it can be quite a problem for small slow boats to get past them. Perhaps with this in mind, rules have been imposed upon the ferry captains stating they must give way to all other river traffic. It is a different matter when you are on the river in a little boat being approached by one of these huge beasts; in reality most vessels give way to the ferries. An acquaintance of mine – following one or two 'near misses' – decided on one occasion to stand up for his rights. Upon finding his boat on a near collision course with a ferry, he stopped his engine right in front of it rather in the fashion of a protester lying down in front of a tank. He was thence seen standing up and waving whilst shouting 'give way, give way!' To his considerable relief the leviathan meekly came to a halt and let him pass. Should all boats adopt this method delays would be very considerable, so he has not repeated the exercise.

As I have said, repeatedly, the Tamar compares favourably with many great rivers of the world in lots of ways. One river would be the River Congo – especially in terms of its fauna. Elephants emerging from lush tropical undergrowth would be rather difficult to imagine at Torpoint. On an average summer's day you would have difficulty detecting a full-sized elephant swimming across the Tamar – but that is not to say it has never happened.

In 1923, Bostock and Wombwell's Circus was crossing the Torpoint ferry. One of its elephants – called Julia – was being used to help load the wagons. The task done, she was tethered for the journey across the river. Unfortunately, she somehow broke free, lumbered to the edge of the ferry, and nosedived (or trunkdived) into the river. Once afloat, she made for the shore which fortunately was not far away; but upon hearing the frantic shouts of her keeper from the ferry, she immediately turned about and began to make for the vessel. As usual the tide was flowing strongly, but the old girl kept at it, and eventually made it across to the other side behind the ferry. The lesson of the story seems to be that the ferry company would probably have been better off using Julia than Jemima.

The number of vehicles crossing the river in recent years has risen considerably. Statistics concerning the modern ferries are quite formidable. Each of the three ferries carries a maximum of fifty-five cars; there are 72,000 crossings of the river per year with a total distance travelled equal to one and a half times round the world. In total 2,500,000 cars are carried in that time. The ferries may not run for very much longer. A replacement bridge has often been talked of, and it probably will not be very long until one is built.

At Torpoint the Tamar has a width of approximately 2,500 feet but, shortly afterwards, the Cornish side of the river opens out into a huge expanse of water called St. John's Lake. At low tide this area dries out to become an enormous mudflat. In the autumn and winter particularly, thousands of probing beaks of wading birds systematically sift through the sediment in search of sustenance. On days when howling winter gales batter the coast at Whitesand Bay a mile or so away, a multitude of gulls and other refugee species from the coast will shelter on the lake. The Dockyard is always within sight, but has little effect upon this backwater where the waters are far too shallow for the Navy to be interested.

At the head of two creeks leading from St. John's Lake stand the villages of Millbrook and St. John's. Millbrook resembles a suburb of Plymouth and is rather unattractive. St. John's, however, remains largely unspoilt and can be reached by small dinghies at high tide by crossing a road ford near the head of the creek. There is a small church tucked away by the waterside, and a little inn – also called the St. John. Both are worthy of a visit.

Stonehouse Pool lies just within the Tamar's domain, being a mere stone's throw from Plymouth Sound. This is an area of considerable contrast: on one side of the pool is the Mayflower International Marina – the usual mix of maze-like pontoons inhabited by all sizes and shapes of yachts with masts and rigging looking more impenetrable than a Brazilian rain forest. On the other side of the pool is the naval victualling yard where, traditionally, ships would take aboard stores before heading out to sea.

The buildings of the victualling yard are far from being only a collection of warehouses. They form the most extensive and grandest facade along the course of the Tamar. Looking almost like a waterside palace, there are two huge wings emanating from a central section fronted by a walled harbour and crowned by an impressive clock tower. Such grand architecture would look just as much at home on the banks of the Thames. In fact the building has been described as one of the best examples of nineteenth century industrial architecture anywhere in England. Accolades for its construction are due to John Rennie, the man also responsible for the creation of Plymouth's breakwater.

Stonehouse Creek is a mere shadow of its former self. It terminates alongside the main Plymouth-Devonport road, less than half a mile from Stonehouse Pool, but in years gone past it snaked inland for more than another mile, ending where Plymouth's Post Office Headquarters building now stands.

It is a pity that Plymouth has systematically filled in the majority

Mount Edgcumbe House stands imposingly at the apex of an avenue of trees leading to the banks of the Tamar.

of its creeks. Of course they were muddy places at low tide, but if they had been dammed off, rather like the creek at Stoke Gabriel on the Dart, Plymouth would have become a city of lakes. Pressure for building land put pay to that idea; consequently, the Tamar has lost hundreds of acres of tributary watercourses with great scenic potential.

From Stonehouse a little passenger ferry crosses to the hamlet of Cremyll. The ferry, inaugurated in the twelfth century, is an anachronism; being the only full time service left on the river catering for foot passengers. In the mid-nineteenth century there were no less than nineteen passenger crossing points on the Tamar between Calstock and the entrance of Plymouth Sound. This ferry has survived because it serves the isolated communities of Millbrook and Cawsand. Cawsand is some two miles distant, but more than five from the next nearest crossing at Torpoint. In the last century the Cremyll ferry catered for horse-drawn vehicles. The table of charges at the time included the following: a hearse without coffin: ten shillings and sixpence; a hearse with coffin: a guinea. In the light of the Tamar's reputation for filling coffins, the owners of the ferry were making a killing – if you will excuse the expression. Until 1844 the ferry connected Devon – not to Cornwall – but to another part of Devon. The parish of Maker had been in Devon's hands from the time of the Saxons who, suspicious of the Celts of Cornwall, had made sure the west side of Plymouth Sound and the Tamar entrance were within their jurisdiction. This resulted in a tiny stream, dividing the twin villages of Kingsand and Cawsand, being the county boundary for more than a thousand years.

During summer weekends the Cremyll ferry is extremely popular with Plymouthians. They stream off the ferry on the Cornish side into the expansive parkland of Mount Edgecumbe (it covers some 865 acres) From Cremyll a long straight drive leads up a gentle slope to Mount Edgcumbe House – the final great house along the Tamar's banks before the sea. The house has a magnificent setting on high ground overlooking the Tamar. Dr. Johnson considered the situation one of the noblest in Britain. Presumably the Grand Admiral of the Spanish Armada, the Duke of Medina Sidonia, did so too. He earmarked the house as his own, following the formality of defeating the insignificant English fleet. The house was a recent construction in those days, having been completed in 1547 in the grand Tudor style. The attempted invasion of the Armada may have been unsuccessful, but another attempted invasion all but totally destroyed the house. In April 1941 German incendiary bombs scored a direct hit, swiftly burning it to the ground. For many years the house's shell stood forlornly at the end of its impressive drive. In 1958 the decision was made to reconstruct it. Over subsequent years the building has been lovingly restored to its original Tudor design.

The banks of the Tamar at Mount Edgcumbe are adorned, once more, with gardens. Each garden has been given the theme of a particular country; there are Italian, French, and English gardens, each with their own distinctive flora. The English garden has such species as the Cork Oak, the Maidenhair tree, and the Handkerchief tree (not to be sneezed at – perhaps they should grow them at Launceston). Camellias abound throughout Mount Edgcumbe; over a thousand were given to the park by the Camellia Society in 1976. Mount Edgcumbe Park is a splendid place to visit, but a spring or autumn visit is recommended. In mid-summer the house and gardens (all open to the public) are overflowing with visitors, most of whom seem to be cluttering up the garden in a state of semi-undress or are seen propelling armies of push chairs up the main drive. In these circumstances the spirit of Tudor England is rather hard to conjure up.

Opposite the landing pier at Cremyll a sign marks the start of a delightful footpath which follows the Tamar towards Millbrook. For a mile the path hugs the river bank and encounters the little harbour at Empacombe – a little used anchorage where time appears to have stood still. Half a mile onward the path joins a road which can be followed further toward Millbrook. At Anderton a footpath to the left climbs a steep hill and eventually reaches Maker Heights where a stunning panorama of the Tamar's lower estuary, its side creeks and the sprawling suburbs of Plymouth stretch for many miles below you. On clear days the view extends to the Saltash bridges, Kit Hill, and far beyond to the north. From Maker Heights the road can be followed to the village of Kingsand. Turning north-east, a footpath following the coastline affords splendid view of Plymouth Sound and eventually returns the walker to Cremyll through Mount Edgcumbe Park. The circular walk covers in total about six miles and uniquely contrasts the Tamar's gently rolling landscape with the bracing saltiness of the coastline.

Plymouth Sound is very close now; with it, the sovereignty of the Tamar is extinguished. The spirit of the river, though, remains undaunted to the end. At Cremyll, Tamara, for the last time, gathers the hills around her in a final gesture of defiance to the sea. The Tamar, unlike many other great rivers, does not meekly surrender its throne to the sea at the mouth of a huge estuary where the dividing line between river and sea are indistinguishable; neither does the river split into a delta where numerous small distributaries are snapped up mercilessly by the ocean. No, the Tamar remains united and distinguishable until the last yard of its existence. Ultimately it bursts forth into Plymouth Sound in a final heroic struggle seen in a cauldron of swirling currents clashing and shattering into a thousand eddies topped by a confused maelstrom of warring wavelets.

The battle is not over immediately, there are skirmishes between the waters of the Tamar and the sea for some distance beyond the mouth. Local skippers know well the furious currents and eddies marking the battle lines between Tamar and sea at spring tides. Their concern has been reflected in the naming of the place where the river meets Plymouth Sound/Devil's Point. No vessel is safe; in the days of sail many a ship was washed helplessly onto the shore's rocky margins. Even today's leviathans are not immune; a while ago, the mighty aircraft carrier *Ark Royal* scraped the rocks close to the river entrance and was not far from being the Tamar's largest casualty. Suddenly, the last rearguard action is over; with the deepening of water past the rocks known as the Bridge the Tamar's waters are finally exhausted and vanquished, swallowed up by the immeasurable legions constituting the English Channel. The spirit of Tamara has finally succumbed, her waters becoming merely a segment of those making up Plymouth Sound. Beyond, on a falling tide, they mingle in ever-reducing minority until at last they are infinitessimal.

The Tamar may have lost the battle, but the war is a perennial one. For as long as howling Atlantic gales send raging rain squalls thundering over the coast onto the bleak moorland of North Cornwall, as long as fresh summer showers moisten the lush pastures and water meadows of rural Devon, as long as a thick autumnal drizzle silently falls on peaceful reed-filled corners of placid creeks, there will always be the River Tamar – surely a Great Little River.

BIBLIOGRAPHY

Baring Gould: *Devonshire Characters*, 1908

W. Best Harris: *Place Names of Plymouth Dartmoor and the Tamar Valley*, W. Best Harris

Frank Booker: *The Industrial Archaeology of the Tamar Valley*, 1967

Frank Booker: *Morwellham*, Dartington Amenity Research Trust, 1970

A.E. Bray: *Sketches of Devonshire on the Borders of Tamar and Tavy*, W Kent and Co., 1838

K.V. Burns: *The Devonport Dockyard Story*, Maritime Books, 1984

Raymond B. Cattel: *Under sail through South Devon and Dartmoor*

Mary Coate: *Cornwall in the Great Civil War and Interregnum 1642-1660*, Bradford Barton 1963

Patrick E. Coleman: *Calstock*, Eco South West, 1984

Joan and Terry Doyle: *Tamar Valley Traveller*, Cornish Safari Company, 1978

Anne Eade: *Kit Hill Our Hill*, Columbian Press, 1989

H.P.R. Finberg: *Devon and Cornwall Notes and Queries* Vol. XXIII p.299, James Townsend and Sons, 1949

H.P.R. Finberg: *Tavistock Abbey*, David & Charles, 1969

Sarah Foot: *The River Tamar*, Bossiney Books, 1989

Helen Harris and Monica Ellis: *The Bude Canal*, David and Charles, 1969

C. Henderson and Henry Coats. *Old Cornish Bridges and Streams*, Bradford Barton, repr. 1972

P.C. Hull: The History of the Cremyll Ferry, *Old Cornwall*, Vol. 7, Camborne Printing Co., 1963

Jack Kingston: *The History of the Torpoint Ferry*.

Alan Kitteridge: *Passenger Steamers of the River Tamar*, Twelveheads Press, 1984

Ian Merry: *The Shipping and Trade of the Tamar* (Part One) Maritime Monographs and Reports, No.46, National Maritime Museum, 1980

H.T. Lenton & J.J. Colledge: *Warships of World War II*, Ian Allen 1973

David Norman and Vic Tucker: *Where to Watch Birds in Devon and Cornwall*, Croom Helm, 1984

R.T. Paige: *The Upper Tamar Valley a Century Ago*, Dartington Amenity Research Trust, 1984

Nicholas Pevsner: *Buildings of England*, Volumes on *North Devon, South Devon and Cornwall*, Penguin

T.C. Pridham: *Devonshire Celebrities*, Henry Seland, 1869

P.E.B. Porter: *In and Around Saltash*, 1905

Joan Rendell: *Along the Bude Canal*, Bossiney Books, 1979

Joan Rendell: *The Bude Canal*, Stannary Press, 1987

Joan Rendell: *Parish Album of Werrington*, Columbian Press 1990
A. L. Rowse: *Cornwall*, Weidenfield and Nicholson, 1988
K & S Spalding: *The Tamar Lakes*, Pub. K. & S. Spalding, 1986
The Tamar Journal: The Morwellham Recreation Co.; articles by R.J. Dyer, D.G. Hull and R.J. Dyer, A. Patrick, R.Pymm, J. Raxworthy, G.A. Rowe, R. Tully, J. Waldon, G. Woodcock.
Arthur Bate Venning: *The Book of Launceston*, Barracuda Books, 1976
Roger Warren: *The Torpoint Ferry: a History And Review*, Tamar Bridge & Torpoint Ferry Committee, 1991
Western Daily Mercury, 2/7/1878
Western Morning News, 19/7/1985, 9/5/1963, 7/1/1970, 20/7/1963
Ralph Whitlock: *Folklore of Devon*, B.T. Batsford, 1973
Graham Wills: *Devon Estuaries*, Devon Books, 1985

Also, with no attributed author:
Antony House, National Trust, 1973
Cotehele House, National Trust, 1982
Landulph Church, Billing and Sons Ltd
A History and Guide to Mount Edgcumbe: House and Country Park, Cornwall County Council and Plymouth City Council.